If Grief Is a Journey, Who Has the Road Map?

A Memoir

By William J. Wilson

For Annie

In memoriam

Other Books by the Author

The Church in Africa (editor)

Paul, The Missionary Pope

The Third World

Say When

With Their Whole Strength

Medicare, Medigap, Catastrophic Care and You (ghostwriter)

Presbyopia: A Practice and Marketing Guide
for Vision Care Professionals

Table of Contents

Table of Contents (cont...)

Foreword

Why write a book about grief? Losing a loved one is terrible enough. Why dredge up the pain of loss, the regret for things said and done or not said and not done? Why spend a year or more regurgitating the loss that destroyed a loving relationship, that imposed a sea change on the rest of your life?

I asked myself these questions early on in the process of planning a book about my loss. No answer was forthcoming, other than an urgent sense that I had to tell my tale. No altruism prompted me to help relieve others' misery. No family member or friend said you have a tale to tell; tell it. No publisher was banging on my door asking for the next bestseller.

This book—rather the first, aborted attempt—came about because I thought writing a humorous account of Annie's loss might assuage my grief. I quickly learned that grief and death aren't funny. The second, complete manuscript developed as a personal act of healing. I felt a need to examine my 43-year relationship with Annie—not to understand it, not to get it all on paper. Rather, I wanted to walk through the milestones of our early relationship and its literal demise. I thought this gentle stroll through memories of a cherished love might give me solace and peace, might show me that loving this marvelous woman had made sense and had been worth the effort both of us put into our meeting and marriage.

Here's our story. The action is taken. The result, like the love of my life, is out of my hands.

PART 1—The Journey

My Story

Triptych 1

Loss

Driving home from shopping on an August Friday,
you collided with fate,
the stop sign on life's highway that awaits us all.
Your car a wreck, your body, too, was all I knew from the call a
state trooper made as I was ready to walk out the door.

My goal—a weekend men's retreat, peace, serenity, friendship,
and fellowship.
Life's goal—pain, uncertainty, and sadness.
Life won. It always does.

The grace, if any there was,
was already mine in the ER of City Hospital before the chopper
whisked you out of my life and me out of your awareness.

I saw you bruised and damaged in the ER,
wrapped in a cocoon of protection;
the swathings hid what you already were and were to become.

Your last words to me were:
"I don't remember what happened."
A mercy for you, that forgetfulness.

Mine to you: "I love you."
A mercy for me, that memory etched forever in my brain
by the acid of grief.
We didn't know, but you had reached the point of no return.
No doctor, no priest, no miracle-working saint could save you.

While the ER surgeon was buying time, your body was slowly
leaking what little time remained through the hourglass of a
trauma too harsh to be reversed.

This became all too clear a few days later at Ruby Memorial
Hospital in Morgantown.
We could keep you on life-support, the doctor explained,
but lack of oxygen was slowly starving your brain.
You were dying.

I must give you one last gift:
Let you die if die you must.

"Give us a few minutes," I said, grateful for a doctor
who didn't whitewash the truth or force a decision.
A kiss. A few private words. Goodbye.
The intubation stopped.
Four days later, your heart stopped.
You ended your transit through this world.

And so, you went and never came back.
Neither has my sense of wholeness, of two being one, of a
soulmate found and held close.

You have gone wherever we go.
Priests tell us one thing, skeptics another.
You are gone, except as a cherished memory.

Will we meet in the sweet by-and-by?
It matters little.
What matters is that we met in the sweet here-and-now.
You gifted me your caring, your humor,
your extroverted greeting of all you met.
You tolerated my moods, my procrastination, my self-seeking.

You are gone; I am left behind.
If you know anything, you know peace.
I know what has been, what it was like,
and what life has become without you.

It will get easier, I know.
It is already, slowly getting easier.
But it will never be easy.

Rescue

I didn't know how lost I was, how much I needed to be found.
Friends close by knew.
Family—yours and mine—farther away knew.
Faithfully, collectively, they set out to rescue my lost soul.

Caring people wrapped me in the warmth of their love.
I'm not used to that.
I'm a giver, not a taker.

The Bible says it is more blessed to give than to receive. Maybe.
It sure as hell is harder to receive,
to take what you need when you need,
to smile and say "Thanks" when a friend or relative
invades the private circle of your loss.

Somehow, way down in the depths of my sorrow,
I knew I'd have to find my way back,
to clasp the proffered hands
and let them lead me back into the sunshine.

I wanted to dig a hole, jump in, and pull the hole on top of me.
I had never felt such misery, such loss, such bewilderment.
Having felt it, owned it, I didn't want to release it.

But they—family, friends, casual acquaintances— forced me to
leave this bereft, dark place to which I had retreated.
They would not withhold their insistent consolation,
their compassion, their empathy.
I wanted to refuse the help proffered. They wouldn't let me.

Slowly, guided by the unflinching gift of their caring, I found my
way into the light.
It was a different light than I had known, dimmer, softer, more
diffuse.

Life won't go away just because we refuse to let it in was the
message their kindness spoke.
Annie cared. People still care. We care.
And you had better start caring again, or you will die inside from
your refusal to receive what those who love you are holding out.

The message somehow got through.
I trudged back into the sunlight of the spirit.
I managed a smile, even a laugh.
Then I managed a second, a third.

Love and laughter.
Two life rings tossed by those who looked for me in the dark sea of loss.
Two life rings I had barely enough strength and willingness to grasp.
Two life rings they used to pull me to safety, to life, to their outreaching hands.

I was rescued.
Not because it mattered to me.
Not because I wanted to be.
Not because I cared.
But because I mattered to them.

Recovery

We mend.

Even if we don't intend to. Even if we don't want to.
Time fixes us…sort of.
I thought I'd never recover,
never learn to live bereft of you,
never build anything that would amount to a life worth
inhabiting.

But I did. I have.

Moving from West Virginia to Alabama opened a door.
The nearness of family, new friends, new activities
all contributed to recovery and reconstruction.
Reconstruction was not good for the South.
But it was good for me in the South.

They say Alabama means "tribal town" in Creek
or "thicket clearers" in Choctaw.
I have been accepted into a new tribe in this town;
I am slowly clearing the thicket of my shattered life,
rooting out the thistles and briars grief has planted in me.

Moving on, entering an enhanced life helps me heal.
In neighboring Georgia, Sherman burned Atlanta.
Your death reduced my soul to ashes.
But we rebuilt, Atlanta and I.
We emerged from our conflagrations new and improved.
New is not always better.
Different does not always improve.
But I am better, stronger. I am, I hope, improved.

Not "new and improved" like laundry detergent.
But stronger in the broken places,
More appreciative of the moment,
the only moment I will ever have.

I could have become a lost soul, a derelict
a wrecked ship on the sands of time.
I didn't.

Those who loved me, new and old, have helped me refuse to
surrender.

"Woe is me" is not my mantra.

Self-pity is not my hiding place.
Surrender is something I don't, won't do.

I have re-entered my life, whatever that may be.
Whatever I may become.

Chapter 1

Meeting—December 1972

What ended as a tragedy had a light-hearted beginning. At Christmastime 1972, Ed Quinn threw a party in Yorkville. All the single or divorced guys I knew on the East Side of Manhattan decided to throw parties. We even convinced all the women we knew to throw parties. Later, Annie would joke that the guys were looking for sex without commitment, and the women were looking for commitment without sex. She was probably right.

Three of us guitar players were performing a Kingston Trio song. I stopped to get a drink from the kitchen. I started to squeeze past an attractive woman I had not yet met. Standing in the doorway, dressed in a long plaid skirt and a beige cashmere sweater, she and my friend Skip were chatting quietly. Her short hair showed the first inklings of gray. She stood with her hip cocked, as though to minimize her lean, five-foot-seven height. Annie, I later learned, would often stand like that. No fool, she knew a sexy pose when she took it.

Skip asked if I knew Anne Huene. I said no, but one look convinced me that I would like to get to know Ms. Huene. Simultaneously, she managed to project sophistication, self-assurance, and an air of bemusement at a world in which she had found her comfort level. Weeks later, I learned that it took a traumatic divorce and several years of self-searching to confer that kind of aplomb.

If I hadn't been, as Skip later told me, a dependency looking for a place to happen, I would not have been so enthralled by this charming, thirtyish woman. Her name, Huene, sounded German, not Bronx Irish. How refreshing to find a female who was not a Celt from Highbridge.

My first marriage to an Irish Catholic had ended disastrously (more my fault than hers, but that's another story). In my bitterness, I resolved never again to make the same mistake. No Irish need apply.

I didn't learn for several weeks that Patricia Anne Dean Huene was, indeed, Bronx Irish. Had I suspected her ethnicity at this first meeting, our love affair would never have gotten too hot not to cool down. Annie looked very "waspy" in her Lord and Taylor outfit. She acted very "waspy." I was completely gulled. I thought I had caught a real live WASP.

Despite her Irish roots, Annie deliberately acted "waspy." She did not want to repeat the fate of her girlfriends: the ones who married the cop from two floors down or the fireman from one floor up.

As they say, if the fish had kept his mouth closed, he'd never have been caught. If I hadn't been looking to break the stranglehold of my own Irish destiny (yes, I am Bronx Irish, too), I would never have succumbed to the classy nurse from East 79th Street by way of St. Nicholas of Tolentine parish.

If you're Bronx, your home parish—not your street, neighborhood, or borough—places you in the Irish Catholic pecking order. Annie's German-sounding last name fooled me into believing that this new woman was "a wealthy WASP from Westchester," as she wished she were. Annie was no more WASP than I was. She was second-generation Irish from Tolentine.

When Skip introduced Annie and me, I didn't realize that this was the beginning of the end or maybe the end of the beginning. Fascinated by one of the most enigmatic females I had ever met, I never got back to my guitar. Poor Tom Dooley never got to hang down his head.

I monopolized Annie for the rest of the evening, ignoring my friend and wingman. Bored at the lack of attention, Skip drifted off, presumably to find another interesting lady. For me, I found Annie plenty interesting—then and, eventually, for a lifetime.

Chapter 2

Courtship

We never had a courtship. We met. Eventually, we dated. Our relationship began when Annie invited me a week later to serve as entertainment at her holiday party. She had only recently moved into her apartment on East 79th Street in Manhattan. She later told me she wanted her 1972 New Year's Eve party to be unique, 100 of her closest friends. "I naively assumed these people would be in my life forever," she later told me. "I even cashed in stock to pay for the party."

Annie had heard me play some folk songs at an earlier get-together thrown by friends a few floors down from her apartment. I remember her sitting on the bed in Dan Fitzgibbons' guest room. As we sang "The Wild Colonial Boy," Annie was the only one in the room besides me who knew all the words. That should have told me something about her ethnicity.

Had I not been singing so loudly myself, I would have also realized that Annie couldn't carry a tune in a tin bucket, a trait that characterizes her entire family. They say love is blind. Maybe it's also deaf, for I was certainly smitten beyond realizing or caring that this lovely woman sang more like a duck than a nightingale.

Enthralled by my voice and guitar virtuosity, I like to think, Annie invited me to perform the same function at her New Year's Eve party a week later. This meant another party and another chance to see Anne Huene. I figured, "Why not?"

New Year's Eve came. We rolled up the rug in Annie's 19th-floor apartment. One hundred of her best friends arrived, and we sang and danced out the old year. Once the new year was appropriately welcomed, everyone left. Looking for a way to ensure I'd see my hostess again, I offered to make Annie breakfast the next morning. She must have wanted to see me, too, because she said she'd be delighted.

Operating on about four hours' sleep, I showed up with orange juice, eggs, bacon, English muffins, and butter at about 9 o'clock. Assuming I was as clueless as most guys, Annie had also gone to our deli and bought orange juice, eggs, bacon, English muffins, and butter.

A superlative cook, Annie could improvise a complete meal with one or two utensils salvaged from her student dorm at

Bellevue Hospital. While she had bought a complete set of new cookware—copper-bottom Revere pots and pans—for her new apartment, Annie had never used them. She performed her culinary magic in one battered aluminum pot and one small cast-iron frying pan from her nursing school days.

Newness presented no problem for yours truly. I scraped the labels off pots and pans and set to work. I hate to cook, probably because I am a lousy cook. But I can make breakfast. So, I fried and toasted and scrambled, and Annie, bless her soul, ate. Breakfast successfully engineered, I told her I had a meeting with some friends uptown, pecked her on the cheek, and exited, her kitchen sink filled with dirty, no longer new Revere Ware.

Beating a hasty retreat from the combined debris of a New Year's Eve party and a holiday brunch is not the recommended way to launch a courtship, but it worked for me. Our relationship did pan out. Annie let me into her life, a life she had been carefully protecting against male encroachments since her divorce.

I later learned that she didn't eat most foods—including just about everything I had placed on the brunch menu—and that she consumed very little of what she did eat. That meant I had two strikes against me at our first shared meal. Fortunately, the third strike never was called.

We fell in love. We lived together. We got engaged, sort of. We had both been down the aisle before. We both knew that "I do's" gained their strength from the commitment behind them. Vows are no more permanent than an unknowable future permits.

I never proposed to Annie. After we started living together, we simply assumed we would marry after my divorce became final. In the No Man's Land between separation and divorce, I kept my fifth-floor walk-up apartment down the block from Annie's building—because we wanted to shelter our mothers from the knowledge that we were "living in sin" (assuming it worked), and also to create a special place for my two young daughters, Claire (8) and Jennifer (4).

I bought a ring as a sign of our commitment. She never wore it. Was I bothered? No. I gave the ring to show my love. Annie took it because she loved me. But the love rested in her heart and mine, not on the fourth finger of her left hand.

Chapter 3

The Wedding—September 1974

We wed most unusually for two Bronx Irish Catholics: hitched by a Unitarian cleric in the United Nations chapel. No spires, no vigil lights, no incense, no tabernacle.

Annie wanted a fancy wedding. Her first union took place at Trinity Church, an Episcopal landmark on Wall Street, with only the groom and his father in attendance. Her folks, devout Catholics, wouldn't attend a "Protestant" wedding. No one from Annie's family showed up. Annie made up her mind that this would not happen the second time around.

Me, I would have settled for a Justice of the Peace or a City Hall clerk. Annie had already received the annulment of her union with husband No. 1. Still unannulled, I had no particular desire to be annulled and didn't plan on being annulled. Hence, we had no thought of a "Catholic" wedding.

I believed, and still do, that it doesn't matter much to man or God how a couple pledges their lives to each other. What counts, what matters, is two hearts agreeing to be one, two minds willing to think, not in unison, but in tandem.

But ... back to the wedding. Mel Hawthorne, the U.N. chaplain, would perform the service. My closest friend, Tom McQueeney, acted as best man. Annie's sister, Mary Margret (yes, if you're Bronx Irish, you use both names) Brennan, was matron of honor.

While Unitarian cleric worked OK for us, Mary Margaret, a shrewd judge of people, particularly mothers, suggested adding a priest to the mix. He could give a blessing after Mel did the service. Mary Margaret knew, and probably still does know, all the clergy of consequence in the New York metro area, so naturally, she landed a priest.

We told Mel about the concluding priestly blessing. "He can do the whole service if you want" was his suggestion. "Oh, no," we said in unison. "We're just doing this to keep our mothers happy!"

We were married to the strains of "Today, while the blossoms still cling to the vine." I was hers; she was mine; our bond was soul deep. We might be legally bound, but no law would ever bind us. Caring and a commitment that transcended contracts or documents fused us, things that Annie laughingly referred to as "here-to-for, where-to-for B.S." There was no B.S. in our union. Later in our marriage, when Annie became a licensed counselor, she refused to acknowledge the word "codependent." Her mantra was interdependent.

We respected each other's autonomy for the next 41 years. Each year lived one day at a time. Each night purposefully sealed with a kiss and "I love you." That must be a record, that "I love you." We gifted each other those words every night. They weren't always spoken trippingly on the tongue. Some nights they came through clenched teeth. But they came. Always.

Our commitment to each other included a determination never to fall asleep locked into anger. Feelings are not facts. We might be angry, but we would never let negative emotions put a period to the end of our day.

Chapter 4

The Crash—August 14, 2015

That's how life began for Annie and me. Neither of us could see how it would end 43 years later. But end it did.

On August 14, around 2 p.m., my life was torn in half by a phone call from a state trooper.

"Are you Bill Wilson?"

"Yes, I am."

"Is your wife, Patricia Anne Wilson?"

"Yes, she is."

"I'm afraid your wife has been in an accident, and she's pretty banged up."

The trooper explained that the crash had occurred in front of Tomahawk Middle School on WV 9 in Hedgesville, West Virginia, about eight miles from The Woods, a retirement community where we had lived for the last 12 years.

On her way back from shopping, Annie never made it home. She will never make it home again. Her Chevy Sonic had collided head-on with a Chevy Trailblazer when her car veered into the oncoming lane.

The Sonic's safety features had performed as designed. The airbags deployed and prevented Annie from hitting the windshield. The engine dropped down, rather than slam back into the front seat. The crumple zones collapsed as planned.

The safety mechanisms had killed my wife. Almost anorexically thin and plagued by pain for more than ten years and having undergone seven back surgeries, Annie didn't carry any excess weight. Her original 136 pounds had faded to about 115. When friends expressed concern. Annie tried to gain weight. She couldn't. As a result, when two vehicles collided at a combined speed of 100 mph or so, she had no adipose tissue to cushion the impact. By saving her life, her car had killed her.

Immediately after I hung up the phone, a friend called. Mary Everhart had been driving to Martinsburg from The Woods to do some shopping. She had arrived right after the accident, even before the paramedics.

"Anne's had an accident."

"I know. I just spoke to the trooper. I'm on my way."

"Don't come on Rt. 9. Traffic's already backed up. Take Lewinsville Rd."

Before heading into town, I called my friends the Ramseths. "Annie's been in an accident, and I need to drive into the hospital. Can you take care of the pets?"

Without hesitation, Chuck replied, "How soon do you need us to be there?" Chuck and Jane arrived, and I headed into town.

By the time I reached the crash site, Annie had been taken by ambulance to the ER at Berkeley Medical Center in Martinsburg. A mangled red sedan gave mute witness to the terrible event that had sent Annie to the hospital.

When we got to Berkeley Medical Center, the ER doc told me Annie had a shattered pelvis, five broken ribs, and a cracked cervical vertebra. Her spleen had been tied off, and she was hemorrhaging in her pelvis. I had one last chance to speak with the woman who had given me her love "until death do us part."

"I can't remember what happened," she said, obviously in shock.

"Don't worry. They're going to take good care of you," I answered. Then, I spoke the last words Annie would ever hear from me: "I love you." It was a fitting, though painful way, to take leave one last time of this woman to whom I had pledged my life.

Mary and I sat in the ER waiting room while Annie was "wrapped like a taco," as the doctor told me, to be medevaced to the surgical shock trauma unit at Ruby Memorial where specially trained surgeons would take care of her injuries.

I stayed home, walked and fed the dogs and cat, and waited for the news the paramedic had promised to phone after the chopper landed.

Chapter 5

Denial Is Not a River in Egypt

"This can't be happening to me!"

When my phone rang that afternoon of August 14, 2015, I was dashing out the door to make a weekend men's retreat with a bunch of guys I had known for years. Not a care in the world.

You know the ad on TV, where the teenager is delighted to find the new car her dad has bought her and the businessman is distraught to see that his car has been vandalized. Both are astonished. Both question what has happened. Both exclaim, "This can't be happening!" Both are told, "It's happening, Baby!" Both end up accepting their respective situations. The teenager with delight, the businessman with great chagrin.

What do Annie's accident and death have to do with a TV commercial for State Farm Insurance? I felt the same as the two individuals in the ad. This can't be happening. Is that my wife on a gurney in the ER? Is she going to be medevaced to Morgantown?

It's not that I didn't know the answer to those questions. I did. It's that I didn't want to deal with the question itself, much less accept an honest reply. To do so would permanently change my life, so I looked for a way to act as if it hadn't happened.

That's denial—a refusal to accept something as plain as the nose on your face. It's what keeps alcoholics and crack addicts in a self-destructive pattern long after their addiction has taken hold and has begun to destroy their lives. It's what keeps an abused wife in a relationship where her husband physically and verbally assaults her regularly. It's what convinces a compulsive gambler that he or she will make it all up on the next roll of the dice or the next trifecta.

Denial doesn't work, never has, never will. But in times of stress and fear, we return to it like the swallows to Capistrano: This time it'll be different. This time I won't get drunk. This time I won't lose my paycheck at the poker table. He didn't really mean to break my arm!

Sadly, denial was just the first bump in the roller coaster ride that soon became my life. Numbness came next. Call it the emotional equivalent of shock, I suppose. Annie, strapped to the gurney, said she couldn't remember what happened in the accident. She may have been on morphine. I wasn't told.

Anyway, her mind (traumatic amnesia?) and her body (physical shock?) were protecting her from experiencing the full impact of what had happened. Good for Annie. She needed that respite.

I wasn't so lucky. I looked at her numbly. She had a few minor scrapes on her forehead, probably from the airbag. If she had been bleeding, the ER staff had already cleaned her up. Her left hand was badly bruised. Later, I learned what I already suspected: three fingers had been broken. Everything else was internal or hidden under the blanket that covered her torso.

Two things hit me like a mallet: awareness of the horrific nature of the damage done to my wife and surprise at how this young doctor could be both casual and compassionate in delivering such awful news.

Chapter 6

Ruby Memorial

That evening around 11 o'clock, I got a call from a male doctor whose name I didn't get.

"Your wife is still bleeding internally. We need your permission to give her more blood." Of course, I gave my OK.

The next morning, Saturday, around 6:30, Doctor Bailey, the chief trauma surgeon, called. "Was your wife responsive when you saw her in Martinsburg?" she asked. When I said that Annie had been aware and responsive, Doctor Bailey told me that Annie had become increasingly less responsive during the night and that the trauma team was not able to get any reaction at all from her in the morning. She said they would keep my wife on a morphine infusion and see what developed. I made arrangements for Annie's and my friend, Ann Gephart, a nurse like my own Anne, to drive me to Morgantown.

Ann drove for two hours through the beautiful Maryland and West Virginia countryside, and eventually, we reached Ruby Memorial Hospital. I am not a medical person. I don't understand medical stuff, and I don't like hospitals. Ann had spent her entire career in hospitals. They did not intimidate her. She knew how to navigate the labyrinth of halls and corridors to reach our goal—the Surgical Shock Trauma Unit on the fifth floor of Ruby Memorial. The sight that was waiting for us made my blood run cold.

Annie lay stretched out beneath white coverlets. Tubes of various sizes and lengths linked her to an array of blinking and beeping monitors. The lights and numbers meant something to the staff and Ann. To me, they just looked like a scene from *ER* or *Chicago Hope*—except that my wife's body was on the business end of all the plumbing.

Annie had been intubated, not because she couldn't breathe on her own according to the doctor on duty, but to keep her airway from collapsing. Pale and inert, she did not look anything like the woman I had known for 43 years.

Annie was not designed to lie comatose in a hospital bed. For most of the time we had been together, she was a perpetual-motion machine. If anyone had ants in her pants, it was Anne Dean Wilson. She could not sit still or remain quiet for more than a few minutes at a time. She once told me, "I tried meditating, but I had to give it up. I just kept having dirty thoughts!"

Patricia Anne Wilson, always Annie to me, was a late-blooming over-achiever. By her own admission, boys were more important than books in high school and even in nursing school. When she did earn her RN from NYU after training at Bellevue Hospital, Annie turned out to be a natural. So much so, that she served as head nurse on two different units while still in her twenties. Private practice and industrial nursing followed. Then, Annie switched careers and earned a certificate as an employee assistance counselor in 1978.

When my job moved us to Washington, D.C., Annie stayed behind and finished her courses at South Oaks Hospital on Long Island. Then she moved to Northern Virginia with me and signed on as a nurse-counselor on the Detox Unit of Washington Hospital Center. She was as good at this new career as she had been at nursing.

When Annie trained at Bellevue, the school gave only an RN. When Annie applied for a head nurse's job at Washington Hospital Center, she lost to someone with a BSN. Undaunted, Annie returned to school.

The hospital had a continuing education program with George Washington University. She earned a bachelor's degree, with a 3.7 GPA, while working full time and being married to yours truly, no small challenge. "I found out my brain still worked," she later told me.

Then she lost out on another promotion to someone with a Master's in Social Work. Back to school again, this time to Trinity College as a member of the inaugural graduating class earning Master's Degrees in Employee Assistance Counselling.

Two things in Annie's college and post-graduate careers impressed me. Writing did not come easily to her. She thought, spoke, and wrote the language of nurse's notes: nouns, concrete adjectives, and an occasional verb. A master manipulator, Annie tried to convince me to write her papers.

"If you love me, you'll write this paper," she whined as she tried to con me into bailing her out during her undergraduate years. "I love you, so I will not write that paper. I'll teach you how to write it." And teach her I did. My years as an adjunct English instructor of freshmen at Northern Virginia Community College had refined my skills at teaching composition. I taught. Annie learned. Then, because her typing skills were abysmal, I typed every paper she wrote for the next five years.

28

What also astonished me about Annie's post-graduate studies was that she talked every single professor at Trinity but one into assigning projects rather than term papers. "That's impossible," I told her when she informed me she did not need to write end-of-semester papers. "When I got my Master's at St. John's, I had to write at least one major paper a semester! How did you do that?"

"Well," she replied with a wry smile, "I convinced my instructors that adults learn by doing, not by studying theory. I guess my arguments were convincing."

Chapter 7

Life Support

Ann Gephart looked at the chart, talked with the doctor and the charge nurse, and translated the information for me into plain English. It seems the medical staff didn't know why Annie had lapsed into a coma. They would run more tests, including an EEG (electroencephalogram) to see what was going on in her brain. Meanwhile, the internal bleeding seemed to have stopped. She was receiving morphine, fluids, and nutrients, but no more blood.

I held Annie's right hand and tried to make sense of the entire situation. The hand was soft, smooth, and surprisingly warm. The broken fingers of the left hand, resting on the coverlet, appeared swollen and bluish. The shock-trauma staff had been so busy trying to keep Annie alive they had little time for minor details like fractured phalanges. During the next few days, we would also learn that Annie had a badly fractured left femur. That, too, was medically insignificant, given her comatose state.

As I sat looking at my unconscious wife, my glance fell to her feet, which were projecting from under the covers. Annie was retaining fluid. Her ankles were badly swollen. With a bizarre sense of irony at the situation, I remembered how frequently Annie would ask me if her ankles were fat. She was obsessed, of course, with the possibility of showing weight gain anywhere in her body. I am no fool. "Your ankles are fine," was my regular answer.

An hour or so later, Ann had learned and interpreted for me all the information the medical staff could give us. Since Annie was in her unconscious bubble and receiving the care she needed, Ann and I headed back to The Woods. We would repeat this sad journey four more times over the next 10 days, never again to see Annie blink an eye or hear her whisper a word.

I made some phone calls to family and friends. My sister and her husband in Hackettstown, New Jersey, were compassionate, but age and distance prevented them from offering much more than sympathy. My niece in Southern California was extremely sympathetic. She had lost her mom, my older sister, a year earlier. But Deirdre could do little from three thousand miles away.

The calls to Annie's siblings could not have been more reassuring. I had seen close-knit families torn apart by sickness and death. The Dean clan reacted as generously as I could have hoped.

Jim Dean, Annie's oldest brother, had suffered a stroke several years earlier, and his wife, Peggy, sheltered him from any upsetting news. Peggy offered her sympathy and prayers, promising to tell Jimmy what had happened when she felt he could handle it. She also offered to do whatever she could.

Mary Margaret Dean Brennan, Annie's kid sister in Avon, New Jersey, was warm and encouraging. Mary and Anne had worked hard at sustaining the bond of sisterhood through the twists and turns one meets on the bumpy highway of life. "Whatever happens, whatever you have to decide," she told me, "please know that we will support you one hundred percent." Mary had just given me the greatest gift I could have asked for: unconditional love and empathy.

Chris, Annie's second brother and the sibling she was probably closest to emotionally said he and his wife Nancy would head east from Michigan as soon as possible. That was no surprise. Over many years, Annie and I maintained a close relationship with the Michigan Deans, as we called them.

"Just tell us where Anne is," Chris had said, "and we'll be there." I offered hospitality, which he declined. "We'll find someplace where we can be near the hospital. Don't worry about us. We'll take care of ourselves." And they did. They also took care of me, demonstrating once again why Annie and I considered Chris and Nancy as much friends as relatives.

Chapter 8

Decision Time August 19, 2015

Ann Gephart and I made two more trips to Morgantown before Chris and Nancy arrived at the hospital. Each visit showed no improvement. Each medical conference showed a baffled trauma team struggling to find out why they couldn't bring Annie out of her coma.

As hours lapsed into days, the frustrated doctors ran more tests. Finally, on our third visit on Wednesday, August 19, Doctor Bailey led Ann and me into a small conference room near the entrance to the shock trauma unit.

She slipped a piece of film into a lightbox on the wall and began explaining what a second, more detailed, EEG had revealed. Annie had suffered a non-hemorrhagic stroke. The doctor pointed to a slightly darker area on the cross-section of my wife's brain.

"This tissue is being starved for blood. Blood clots have blocked the flow of blood to your wife's brain, killing these cells. Her brain is slowly dying."

I looked at my friend Ann. Far more accustomed to dealing with these baffling medical issues than I, she nodded in agreement with the doctor. The verdict was in. Two people I respected—Doctor Bailey for her medical expertise and Ann Gephart for her love of Annie and me—had delivered and confirmed a verdict I had hoped would never come. Annie was going to die. And it would be up to me to decide when.

Doctor Bailey explained that if I wanted to prolong Annie's life, I could. However, she would need to be moved to long-term intensive care. "We need the bed as new cases come in." Then, she pointed out that, if I wanted Annie to be on life support, that would only be possible out of state. "West Virginia has no facilities capable of delivering that kind of care. Also, with her five broken ribs, your wife is incapable of breathing deeply enough to supply the oxygen her organs need to live. She will eventually die from organ failure."

How doctors can deliver such awful news baffles me. I appreciated how this skilled surgeon gave Ann and me the unvarnished truth. She did not minimize or dramatize the information she was imparting. She did not steer me in any direction—for or against taking Annie off the ventilator.

That didn't make my decision any easier or less painful. But it did make it clearer.

Annie and I had often talked about our unwillingness to be kept on life support, about our dislike of any extraordinary measures to prolong a life that was coming to an end. We each had living wills and medical powers of attorney. I knew what had to be done. I knew what she would have wanted to be done. And I knew the decision was mine alone.

"My wife's brother is driving from Michigan and should arrive tomorrow. Can we at least keep her on life support until he and his wife get here?" I asked.

"Of course. You will need to tell me when you are ready to have us remove the ventilator."

That was it. No fuss. No muss. Just accepting the inevitable and making arrangements to have it happen.

Chapter 9

Preparing for the End

I knew Annie would die, and soon. I knew because that was the decision I had just made on her behalf. The next step for Ann Gephart and me was to find a funeral home and make arrangements for them to receive Annie's body and carry out the cremation she had wanted for her final disposal.

Finding a funeral director, even after the hospital social worker gave me the name of Hastings Funeral Home, proved to be quite a challenge. Morgantown, besides being the home of West Virginia University, is an old mining town. Many of the buildings predate the Twentieth Century. The part of town Ann and I scoured to find Hastings Funeral Home was old, shabby, and badly in need of gentrification.

I have a friend who graduated from WVU. When I told Doug that our search for a funeral director had convinced me that Morgantown was a dump, his reply was: "It was a dump when I went there in the Sixties. It was a dump when dad went there in the Thirties. And it was a dump when grandfather went there before World War I." So much for family traditions.

Ann and I kept getting lost in our quest for the funeral home. We couldn't find any street signs. Eventually, we stumbled upon the two-story building by accident. The receptionist, looking like a character from *Mayberry R.F.D.*, handed us a packet of forms and offered coffee, which we declined. Eventually, Dan Hastings, the funeral director and one of the owners of the business, took us into his office and briefed us on what needed to be done.

If the receptionist was Aunt Bee, Dan was a cross between Willy Loman and Rodney Dangerfield. His explanation of what had to happen after Annie passed away, how he would claim her body, and the necessary preparations for her cremation was part sales spiel and part stand-up comedy. When we told Dan that we had a difficult time locating his building, he light-heartedly told us that locations were hard to find in Morgantown because the students routinely stole the street signs to adorn their frat houses. They pilfered so many signs that the town fathers finally stopped replacing them.

Annie was still on life support when we first met with Dan. We needed to find out when he would enter the picture, what he would do, what the coroner would do, what the hospital would do, and what we would need to do. He kept our discussion light, peppering it with jokes and quips. At first, I was growing angry at his irreverence, but then it dawned on me that Dan's patter was designed to keep Ann and me from totally falling apart. He pretty much succeeded.

I could see the irony in his seriocomic description of the chain of events that had to unfold before he could claim Annie's body and deal with her cremation. On Thursday, August 20, I signed the authorization for taking possession of Annie's body and carrying out the cremation.

Annie probably would die over the weekend or early the next week. Nothing happens anywhere that I have ever been on weekends. Timing is everything. You may die on a Friday if you want, but don't plan on having your burial until sometime late the following week.

Annie first had to die, he told us. Then the coroner had to be found. "I have no idea where he'll be over a weekend." The implication was that this guy could be fishing, visiting his grandkids, passed out drunk on his kitchen floor—or anywhere in between.

Even if Annie had the grace to die on Saturday or Sunday, the funeral director made it clear that he didn't know when the medical examiner could fit generating Annie's death certificate into his busy schedule, assuming he could be located. Had I not been in the no man's land between heartbroken and numb, I might have seen the humor in Annie's refusal to expire more conveniently.

"Do you want to look at some urns?" he asked, abruptly changing the subject. Ann and I looked at each other, realizing that taking care at least of this part of the funeral arrangement might save us four hours on the road in an additional round trip to the Eastern Panhandle. So, we went to the display room to choose an urn.

King Tutt's tomb could not have looked more resplendent when Howard Carter and Lord Carnarvon first tiptoed into the crypt than did Hastings Funeral Home's display of caskets, urns, and other funerary paraphernalia. For the first time since Annie's crash, the thought of what this would cost entered my mind. I knew Annie wanted a simple funeral and burial. We had discussed this along with our preferences for end-of-life medical care. What I did not know was that the funeral business had gone green along with the rest of the country.

"You're planning to bury Mrs. Wilson, correct?" Dan asked.

"Yes. We already have a plot in the cemetery at Hedges Chapel in our community." I didn't bother to tell him that choosing cremation had saved money—smaller remains meant a smaller, less expensive plot in the graveyard of our 150-year-old community church.

"Well, you don't want a bronze or marble urn. They don't decompose after burial. We have here an urn that is recyclable," he told us, picking up a vessel that looked straight out of the Elgin marbles or an ode by Keats. "This," he explained, "is made of compacted salt. It will be reabsorbed after burial along with your wife's ashes."

The undertaker's aplomb while going all environmental on us was rather disconcerting. However, the knowledge that Annie's ashes could rejoin Mother Earth was a consolation, and the knowledge that I did not need to seek irrelevant immortality through an unnecessarily large expense was reassuring. Maybe I was simply becoming as surreal as Dan's sales spiel.

I authorized removing life support on Friday, August 21. Not knowing how long it would take for Annie to breathe her last, Chris and Nancy Dean, Ann Gephart, and I each spent a few quiet, private moments with Annie's still form. I don't know what the others said, nor did I expect them to share their final words to this amazing woman who had so differently helped shape our individual lives.

My message to Annie was simple. I told her I had always loved her. I admitted that, as often as I may have failed to be the kind of husband she deserved, I had done my best. I asked her forgiveness for those times, many they were, when I had fallen short of the mark. Finally, I commended her spirit to whoever, whatever, might be waiting on the other side. I kissed her pale, dry forehead, and left the room so that Chris and Nancy could be with their sister.

As I waited for Annie to die, I stayed home and cared for my pets. Had she been responsive, I probably never would have returned to The Woods. Since Annie could not know I was there and I could not know when her end would come, it made more sense to be where three innocent critters needed me than to stay when I could do or say absolutely nothing to ameliorate the situation in Morgantown.

Several times a day, I called—on Friday, Saturday, Sunday, and Monday. The nurse assured me that the staff was keeping my wife comfortable and that she would let me know when any change occurred.

Finally, around 11 p.m. on Monday, the phone rang. The nurse gave me the news I both dreaded and hoped for: Annie had stopped breathing shortly before the phone call.

Chapter 10

First Things First

When I lost Annie, I was baffled by many situations. Until she left, I was on top of the world, master of my fate, captain of my soul. At least I thought so. Backstopped by a smart, highly competent wife with an A-type personality, I never had reason to think differently. Then the walls came crumbling down.

Annie was gone. The engine that powered my sense of competence and relative omnipotence had died, literally. I was lost and not yet found, and there were beasties in the dark wood in which I found myself. Among them:

I didn't know what to expect, how to handle myself, or anything that might happen as Annie's lifeless body lay in the surgical trauma unit of Ruby Memorial Hospital.

What I wanted to do was go away or, preferably, have the world go away. I was joining Wordsworth's team: "The world *is* too much with us." I just wanted to get off the daily grind, not see friends, not pick up my routine. Annie's death shattered my life. I was an emotional wreck, a lost child in the madding crowd. I wanted out.

I had seen this need to escape up close when my older sister in California lost her husband. John died, and Margie became a virtual recluse. Except for her adult daughter, she saw no one—no friends, no outside interests, no social activities, no interaction with anyone she could avoid.

She read, almost obsessively. Agatha Christie, Zane Grey, and Louis L'Amour became her surrogate family. When she finished their books, she reread each. How many times, I have no idea. From her example, I concluded that, for me, "opting out" was not an option.

Yet, I was in *terra incognita*. As a reasonably intelligent guy, it had never dawned on me when I got blind-sided by Annie's accident and subsequent death that I wouldn't know what I would feel, what I would want to do or not do, what I would have to do or not do. I soon learned that life didn't stop just because I wanted it to.

When Doctor Bailey told me that my wife was going to die soon, there were very specific, unavoidable consequences I had to deal with. Then Annie did die, and the pieces started to fall into place as I continued to fall apart.

Only then did I begin to fathom just how competent and compassionate the hospital staff was and just how much Dan Hastings' sense of gallows humor had helped Ann and me navigate the Scylla and Charybdis of arranging a funeral over a distance of 131 miles with absolutely no previous experience.

Ann got Annie's urn safely home. The funeral home had packed the urn securely in a large cardboard box, which I left on the dining room table for several days until we could have the funeral Mass. Maybe this was bizarre. It didn't seem so to me, probably because I didn't know what else to do.

I felt no need to talk to the carton. I felt no sense that the ashes nestled inside were Annie's presence trying to reach out to me from The Beyond. I was overwhelmed with grief in a way I had never felt before. I had nobody to tell me what the proper reaction might be. The only tactic I could come up with was to avoid knocking the carton off the dining room table until the day of the funeral.

I didn't know what to do. I suspect that nobody outside the funeral industry gets good at arranging a funeral. Most of us don't get much practice. There certainly is no chance for a dress rehearsal.

What has to be done seemed pretty straightforward, as Dan explained it. So does a reasonably lucid explanation of the rules of cricket. But if you've never played the game, you might as well be arranging a moon shot as cremation and burial. There are legal issues, insurance, transportation of the remains, selection of an urn or casket, planning the funeral, the opening of the grave or disposition of the ashes, to name just the most immediate factors that came into play.

I had to make these decisions. This was my stuff, nobody else's. I could not delegate it. During my professional career, I had always managed to find a smart assistant who liked doing the financial pieces of public relations, much to my boss's chagrin. That skill saved me from having to display my total ineptitude with things arithmetical. Annie had performed the same service in our 41 years of marriage. She actually liked to balance checkbooks and verify credit card receipts.

My legerdemain in eluding family finances meant that I had no idea what to do now, starting with paying for cremation and an urn and opening a grave to receive the ashes. Fortunately, being inept and needy occasionally has its advantages.

My very ignorance drove me to ask competent friends to blaze a trail for me. I felt like the helpless explorer on his first safari. I needed someone to go before me to whack down the brush with his machete. To my good fortune, those people showed on schedule and on-demand, starting with Ann Gephart and Dan Hastings, the merry mortician.

As the days and weeks following Annie's death moved forward, I would learn that relatives and friends wanted to be there for me. I remembered a conversation I had with my good friend Tom McQueeney many years before after his infant daughter had died from crib death. Tom told me how he had stood looking south on Second Avenue in Manhattan. He could see or imagine seeing New York Hospital, the Rockefeller Institute, Cornell Downstate Medical Center, Bellevue Hospital, among others. "It dawned on me then that not all the talent in those medical facilities could help me or my baby daughter. I realized that this was a terrible situation that had to be taken care of. And it was up to me to take care of it."

All things being equal, that's the terrible situation I found myself in as Annie lay dying with a Gordian knot of tubes entering and leaving her shattered body. Her situation had to be taken care of, and it was up to me to do it. I had to learn a host of things so I could figure a way to get my dead wife's ashes safely into her grave at Hedges Chapel.

Within a few days, my daughter Claire arrived from Alabama. In her quietly competent way, she took charge. I had written and placed Annie's obituary in the *Martinsburg Journal*. When it came to preparing the memorial card, I couldn't find any that fit my conception of what Annie would have wanted.

Digging through Annie's papers, I did find a reflection on death that she had stashed in two separate folders. She had heard this reflection read at a funeral more than 20 years earlier and had been so moved that she told me that this was what she wanted to be read at her funeral. Knowing I would forget, she had put copies of the reading in two different places, realizing that I would eventually stumble across at least one.

Claire, a skilled writer-editor and internet sleuth, tracked down a site where she could get the memorial card made, using a picture I had taken of Annie several years earlier. With no help from me, she created a beautiful tribute to her stepmom. That was the most obvious gift Claire gave me and the stepmother she never called other than friend. Words cannot capture the emotional support I gained just from her presence.

In my grief, I failed to realize that Claire was dealing with her sorrow at losing the woman who had frequently told her and her sister, "I'm not your mother. You already have a mother. And I'm certainly not your stepmother. I'm your friend."

And Annie had been indeed a trusted friend to Claire and, when circumstances permitted, to Jennifer. Without wishing to sound chauvinistic, I often felt that Claire and Annie shared a bond as women that I could not aspire to either as a husband or as a father, much less as a mere man. They shared confidences that I never fully entered into, which was fine with me and undoubtedly with them.

I had no way of anticipating the chain of support that had to be mustered to deal with Annie's sudden death. I was blessed that everyone I needed, and I needed a lot of them, was in the right place at the right time. Maybe dealing with death and its consequences is easier after prolonged sickness. Maybe not. My experience doesn't include that type of loss. For me, overwhelmed by catastrophe, family and friends were there when I had to lean on them for love and help.

Chapter 11

Planning the Funeral

Then it hit me. My partner, the focal point of my life, was gone, forever. Things would never be the same. Annie had left me, but the niche her love had carved in my heart would remain. I had lost her dynamic presence, her strength of character, and her ironic sense of humor.

Memories of words spoken, adventures shared would fade. Annie's smile, her warm heart would no longer grace my days. Now came the painful steps of preparing all the things surrounding the funeral, burial, and the other accouterments society asks of those who survive a loss. I alone owned this chore because I was the only adult in the room.

First, I wrote the obituary. I learned that not only does one compose the recapitulation of the loved one's life, one pays the paper to run it. I have read countless sappy reminiscences in the "Irish Sports Pages" over the years. As a professional PR man, I intended that Annie's obit would be factual and would also document a life of accomplishment. Maudlin sentimentality had no place in this woman's life or my summary of it.

Here is what I wrote:

Patricia A. Wilson (1939 – 2015)
Patricia A. "Anne" Wilson of Hedgesville, W.V., peacefully departed this life on Monday, August 24 at 11:00 p.m. She was 76.

A native of The Bronx, N.Y., Anne trained as a nurse at Bellevue Hospital in Manhattan and pursued careers in hospital, private practice and industrial nursing for many years. She later trained as a substance abuse counselor, moved to Washington, D.C., and began working on the Detox Unit of the Washington Hospital Center. At that time, Anne returned to school, earning a Bachelor's Degree in Education at The George Washington University and a Master's Degree in Employee Assistance Counseling at Trinity College. She served as the employee assistance counselor at the Library of Congress and later became the program administrator of the U.S. Senate's Employee Assistance Program. She retired in 2004.

Anne was an active member of St. Bernadette's Catholic Church in Hedgesville, and of the Woods Women's Golf

Association. She is survived by Bill Wilson, her husband of 41 years; her brothers James J. and Christopher M. Dean; her sister Mary Dean Brennan; her stepdaughter Claire M. Wilson; step-grandchildren Lucy and Mary Bolton and Liam McKellips; and by numerous nephews, nieces and grand-nephews and grand-nieces.

Burial will be private. In lieu of flowers, contributions may be made to the Wounded Warrior Project or the North Shore Animal League.

There it was in black agate type: Annie was dead. She would never be alive again. She would never smile. She would never point out that I had once again parked the car catawampus and insist that I realign it. She would no longer storm off when she demanded the car keys after I told her I didn't give a rat's ass how crookedly I had pulled into a space.

Her generosity, her honesty, and her gentle soul would no longer grace my life. She would never again try to give Miss Molly, the cat, a peck on the forehead only to receive a bite on the nose as her reward. Those things were in my memory bank and only there. Togetherness had become aloneness. Companionship had morphed into loneliness. Mutuality had degraded into singularity. With Annie gone, I was alone, sorrowfully trying how to figure out how to make the best of a God-awful situation.

First came preparing for her funeral. Annie's ashes sat on the dining room table. What little remained of my wife did not make me sad or evoke her presence in any particular way. The nine pounds of remains were not Annie. They deserved my care and attention because that was all I had: nine pounds of ashes in a compacted salt urn. A fitting end to a life well-lived? A place to wait until the earth reclaimed what little was left of this vibrant companion who had given me 43 years of love? Poets and songsters may have answers. I didn't. I was just trying to get the ashes from the dining room table to the Hedges Chapel cemetery by way of St. Bernadette's church.

I called Patti Maerten, the administrative assistant at St. Bernadette's. When I tried to explain that Annie had died as the result of a car crash, I broke down and sobbed uncontrollably. Patti, an extraordinarily kind and empathetic woman, waited patiently until I had run out of tears.

She then picked up the thread of our conversation. She invited me to come in to select the music and scripture readings for Anne's funeral and assured me that she would take care of the specifics involved in putting together the service.

The offices and priest's residence for St. Bernadette's are located in a nineteenth-century building known as the Stone House. When I arrived, Patti greeted me with a hug and a sad smile, as did Father Pucciarelli, the retired Marine chaplain who served as the church's priest.

Patti walked me through the service, gave me a list of possible readings and hymns, and let me cry myself dry each time my sorrow overwhelmed me. Then, Father Pooch, as we all called him, asked if I had a few minutes to sit and chat about Annie. Of course, I did. So, we went into the small living room of the Stone House. Father Pooch pulled out a yellow pad and sat, pen poised, ready to hear what I had to say.

I told the priest essentially what I have written in these pages, laundering some of the anecdotes out of respect for his role and adding an occasional anecdote in response to his questions. A few moments turned into an hour and a half, partly because I would break down every few minutes and partly because Annie had led such a rich, varied life that her story inevitably spawned additional tales as it unfolded.

As I cobbled together the facts of Annie's life, I shared with Father Pooch and Patti that Annie and I closed out each day with the words "I love you." We had committed to ourselves and each other that we would not go to bed angry. We had lived up to that commitment. Keeping that promise belonged more to her than to me.

Annie did not make promises lightly. When she said she'd do something, she did it. She also didn't harbor grudges or nurse resentments the way I often did. In fact, by her refusal to let me pout, Annie had helped me achieve modest success in grappling with this character defect.

When I had shed all my tears and dumped all my recollections of Annie, Father Pooch put down his pad with the comment, "There are so many stories here, you should make a movie!" I am no screenwriter, but the life journey of Anne Dean Wilson certainly contained a rich trove of anecdotes. She lived her life, not with gusto, but with energy, honesty, and empathy. Like Will Rogers, Annie never met anyone she didn't like. She had no enemies and a battalion of friends. One or two friends had neglected or dropped Annie over the years. She never could figure out why, but she never stopped trying to draw them back into her circle of intimates.

Chapter 12

The Funeral

The day of the funeral arrived. I got the carton to the church. My friend Acolyte Frank Dobscha and I placed the urn and a photo of Annie in the center aisle just in front of the sanctuary. Father Pooch said the Mass and preached the eulogy.

This Marine chaplain gave a touching farewell sermon, drawing on his friendship with Annie and the protracted conversation we had during my 90 minutes with him and Patti Maarten in the Stone House.

Priests have come under a great deal of disfavor and criticism in recent years, much of it deserved and far too much from me. My experience of Father George Pucciarelli was of a man who was the exception to all the blame that had been heaped on his fellow clerics by a generation of disenchanted Catholics.

Francis X. Winnett, a good friend of mine, had served in the Marines with Father Pooch. A few years before Annie's death, when he and I were discussing that St. Bernadette had recently acquired a new priest, a retired Marine chaplain, Francis asked his name.

"George Pucciarelli."

"He was one of the good ones."

"What do you mean?"

"Chaplains are officers. Most of them hung out with other officers. Pooch hung out with us grunts."

I doubt that any noncom has ever paid a higher compliment to a commissioned officer. Based on my own experience of this very fine man, I do not doubt that Pooch fully deserved it.

The funeral Mass was crowded. My sister Judy and her husband had driven from Hackettstown to be with Claire and me. Just about everyone from Annie's side of the family who could make the trip had shown up. I was reminded then, as I am at most weddings and funerals, how seldom we see those we purport to love and how quickly we make promises to "get together real soon"—promises which we rarely keep.

I had chosen readings and hymns that I knew were Annie's favorites. How odd that we respect the deceased's taste in planning funerals when they are well beyond being consoled or irritated by any choice we make. Of course, the menu of possible selections is replete with old chestnuts, readings and hymns which most of us have heard throughout our lives, so there is almost no chance of missing the mark. I wanted to avoid mawkish sentimentality in my choices, so I picked my favorites. I cherished every selection I had included in the service.

Claire and I sat alone in the front row on the right side of St. Bernadette's, a church for which Annie and I had made and paid pledges for six years to build as a new home for the local faith community. Claire held my hand, off and on, as she sensed I was about to come unglued. I made it through the readings and most of the hymns, but when we sang "Amazing Grace," a spiritual that resonated for both Annie and me because of our personal histories, I choked and almost couldn't finish the song.

Wretches like Annie and me had indeed been saved. While I was still blinded by the limitations of this life, she may have finally reached that stage Paul of Tarsus described where we will no longer see as through a glass darkly. Certainly, at Annie's funeral Mass I had not reached that level of awareness. I could scarcely see through the tears that blinded my eyes.

The funeral service ended, as it always does, with the priest sprinkling holy water on the remains of the deceased. Father Pooch circled the urn, liberally waving the aspergillum like a flyswatter at a summer picnic. Even in my grief, I remembered that the urn was compacted salt. Water dissolves salt, and I feared we were about to witness the birth of a catastrophe. The urn would disintegrate from the water. Annie's ashes would spill on the table and floor. And what on earth would we do?

Well, either the priest's aim was bad or the salt urn was more solidly manufactured than I realized, but my fear did not materialize. Annie got her blessing, the urn remained whole, and the Mass came to a graceful, if not happy, ending.

Chapter 13

The Burial

As we prepared to bring Annie's remains to their final resting place, I didn't trust myself to take the urn in my car. So once again, I called upon Frank Dobscha to perform a final act of service to Annie.

"Could you see that the urn gets to Hedges Chapel? You're the only one I trust to make it happen safely."

"Of course."

Frank boxed the urn in the carton I had brought from Morgantown, bubble wrap and all. He secured it in the front passenger seat of this Chevy Equinox with the seatbelt and slowly drove the three miles to the cemetery.

After we had arrived, I searched for Tim Wall, the gravedigger, to pay his fee. He was nowhere in sight. Finally, I found Tim behind a tree in a remote part of the property. He had that lean, self-sufficient look West Virginia farmers have sported for centuries. "I broke my power jackhammer and my shovel," he told me, "but the hole is dug. I'll fill it in after you're finished with the service." There is more than a little truth to the common saying that West Virginia's main crop is rocks.

Father Pooch blessed the grave and then, at my request, read the reflection Annie had picked out so many years before. I had thought of reading the poem myself, but ultimately realized I would have fallen apart had I tried to do so.

This is the verse, by Theodora Kroebler:

Poem for the Living

When I am dead Cry for me a little.
Think of me sometimes But not too much.
It is not good for you Or your wife or husband
Or your children

To allow your thoughts to dwell Too long on the dead.
Think of me now and again As I was in life
At some moment which is pleasant to recall But not for long.
Leave me in peace
As I shall leave you, too, in peace.
While you live,
Let your thoughts be with the living.

One last sprinkling with holy water and Annie was laid to rest. Had she been there to see how the services were carried out, I hope Annie would have uttered the words she spoke after every funeral, "She was well buried."

Ann and Ron Gephart, who had supported me throughout the two weeks following Annie's accident, had volunteered their home for a post-funeral gathering. I chatted numbly with my sister and her husband and the nephews of the Maher family, with my extended family in the Dean/Brennan clan, and a host of friends who came to honor Annie's memory.

Still dazed by the tragic string of events of the last two weeks, I could not list all who attended. I guess funerals do that. The combination of shock, grief, and information overload cushions us against the awful reality that is ours and only slowly evaporates, allowing life to seep in so that we can do what needs to be done.

Undoubtedly, we say things we would have suppressed had we known what was going to come out of our mouths. We neglect to say other things. We dote too much on some who attend and ignore others.

All of this undoubtedly happened at the Gephart's that afternoon. It struck me that Annie would have loved this kind of party. She considered having 50 or 60 of her closest friends for dinner as little more than a quiet night at home. Only one thing was missing at this gathering—Annie, the guest of honor.

Chapter 14

Home Alone

Annie was buried. That's where it ended. Or started. My wife was dead. The focal point of my life for the previous 43 years lay in a grave in the chapel cemetery. Now I had to figure out how to live my life alone.

Annie's ending had been decided. My new beginning lay entirely in my hands at a time when I could scarcely put one foot in front of another. Too bad. I had to go on. I had to figure out how to build a new life, no matter where I was psychologically and emotionally.

No one ever knows how he'll react to death. We can't anticipate how grief will affect us. I was tempted to become a recluse, to hide, to resign from my life. Not that I wanted to commit suicide. I am too much in love with life and too cowardly to have considered doing myself in. But I was lost in a wilderness of pain and grief beyond anything I had ever experienced.

I would cry, sometimes uncontrollably, at anything that reminded me of Annie and our life together. I lost any desire to eat. Coupled with my distaste for cooking, this was a recipe guaranteed to bring on weight loss. I got so thin so fast that a friend at church asked me: "Are you eating?" I lied and said, "Yes." A more honest reply would have been, "Not much."

How could I find my way out of this awful place? How does anyone face such grief come back? My recovery, if you can call it that, began with doing the next dumb thing.

Certain elements of daily living won't go away just because we want them to. My pets—two Bichons and a cat—gave me a reason to get out of bed every day. Allstate, Comcast, BlueCross and BlueShield, among others, expected to be paid. I needed to pay them unless I was willing to lose the services they and other companies provided.

Wandering the morass of Allstate's phone menu proved less formidable than I anticipated. These people are pros. They deal with accidents and death every day. The staff who handled my case were kind, responsive, and efficient. Without wishing to sound like a TV commercial, I truly was in "good hands."

The funeral day ended. Family and friends left with promises to get together "real soon." Now began my sorrowful journey. Widowhood has no user manual, no timetable. Each of us explores our personal *terra incognita*, hoping we don't get lost—whatever lost means. Each of us counts the sad days, not even considering that we might eventually emerge from this black tunnel, not realizing that a day may come when we don't wake up in a profound state of sadness.

Gus and Sadie kept me moving and focused on their needs. Leashes in hand, I walked the neighborhood three or four times each day, creating an opening where neighbors could stop and chat, occasionally ending our conversations with a dinner invitation or a golf date.

Minimal socializing had become unavoidable. It may have saved me from even greater isolation and more protracted sadness.

Annie and I had lived together for a long time. We shared domiciles, finances, interests, and lifestyles. We could finish each other's sentences, predict each other's tastes and decisions, cherish the same friends and hobbies, carp at each other's faults.

I found Annie a never-ending source of amusement and newness. She pretty much did the same with me. "Whatever else it's been," I often told her, "it has never been boring." As well as I thought I knew my wife, as complete soul mates as we were, Annie would say or do something most days that shattered any preconceptions I might have formed of her personality.

I thought that redoing the kitchen counters had completed Annie's agenda for renovations. Then, one sunny June day after breakfast she told me: "I want to get stone countertops."

"We just did the kitchen last year. It cost a small fortune. We don't need new countertops. Besides, where will you find the money?"

I should have known that raising the cost issue made no sense. It had failed numerous times in the past. Having failed to learn from history, I was about to see it repeat itself.

"I've already saved the money," Annie shot back. Sails aback, becalmed by my own lack of awareness, I had no option but to capitulate. Within a month, Annie had her quartz kitchen counters, fully paid for.

That would be her last home improvement, although neither of us realized it at the time. Months later, as I stumbled through each day after burying her, the counters became a daily reminder of how much change Annie had engineered in our lifestyles, in our homes. Every time I wiped the counter, I thought of Annie. Every time I placed a glass on the counter reminded me of the first time I had set down a wine glass after a dinner party and broken the stem right off it.

Several weeks after her funeral, I found another indicator of how adept Annie was at squirreling away money for a rainy day, or a kitchen counter, or a two-car garage. I decided, out of boredom or loneliness, to clean the top of the refrigerator one morning. Nested together, I found a pair of aluminum bake pans, the disposable kind she often used to make a meatloaf or to bake banana nut bread.

The pans didn't quite nest evenly. When I separated them, I learned why. She had stashed 24 crisp $100 bills in a bank's cash envelope. I never checked the serial numbers, but I bet that they were sequential, that the Benjamins were in mint condition. Had Annie started a slush fund for her next project? I'll never know. The money did come in handy for incidental expenses during the first months of my loss.

Chapter 15

Memorial Service

St. Bernadette has a Bereavement Committee headed by a wonderful woman named Maureen Sabol. I consistently misnamed this group of caring people the Grievance Committee, making our little rural church sound like the focal point of a union action.

Annie joined the committee because she felt that there she could best offer service to our faith community. Unfortunately, she only lived long enough for me to become one of the parishioners to benefit from the hospitality offered by these ladies. Before Annie could serve others, she was served; rather, the committee served others in her honor at the memorial service and luncheon held for Annie in October, some six weeks after her death.

The six-week delay was caused by all-too-human requirements: First, Maureen, the lynchpin of the committee's planning efforts, was on vacation. Then, Father Pooch, who would say the Mass, was off on a trip. This eliminated the rest of August and all of September as a time for family, friends, and neighbors to get together to celebrate Annie's life. Finally, we settled on a time and date: 11 o'clock on October 16 worked for everyone. A luncheon prepared and hosted by Maureen and her fellow committee members would follow the service.

Since the family had made the trek to rural West Virginia in August, I actively discouraged them from returning for the memorial celebration. I tried to let them off the hook gracefully, without creating a sense that they were being excluded.

"This is really for friends and neighbors. You have already paid your respects. Many of you have jobs and kids in school. I think Annie would be the first one to say stay home. So, I'm saying it for her."

St. Bernadette's holds about 150 people. The pews were full for Annie's memorial Mass. People from The Woods, friends and fellow women golfers, members of several organizations Annie belonged to, co-workers and fellow retirees, and many of the friends we had made at St. Bernadette's over the years came to say goodbye to a lady who had touched their lives in a variety of ways. The Mountain Lake Singers, a group I had started and had sung with for many years, provided the music. My fellow musicians—Dave and Kat Cooper and Lee Conlon—remained a source of comfort and strength in the weeks that followed Annie's death.

We opened with "Amazing Grace" because so many of us have found that this hymn beautifully describes our own interior journey. I know Annie had felt, as I did, that John Newton, former slaver and later Anglican clergyman, so effectively summed up how many of us move from wretchedness to redemption. We shared his candid admission that the grace was a gift, not anything we earned.

The readings at the Mass were pretty much the same as one hears at funerals in virtually any Catholic church. The anonymous author of Wisdom assured his fellow Jews in Alexandria, "The souls of the just are in the hand of God…they are at peace." I certainly hoped that he was right, but my own belief is that nobody knows what is on the other side of the veil that separates the living from the dead. We create elaborate metaphors and scenarios to comfort ourselves in times of loss. Maybe they're true; maybe not. They do afford us consolation in our grief, something to cling to when all the lights seem to have gone out.

In the Roman rite, a responsorial psalm follows the first reading of scripture. A cantor sings the verses of a psalm, and the congregation responds with an antiphon, either a verse from that psalm or a reflection on its message. I had made up my mind that I would sing the psalm for Annie and that I would sing her favorite and mine, Psalm 23, "The Lord Is My Shepherd."

Wanting to do something is not the same as doing it. I feared I might not be able to complete the challenge of singing out of love for my dead wife, so I asked Lee Conlon, my co-tenor and soloist, to jump in and finish the psalm if I broke down. Fortunately, I made it to the end. Lee later teased me that I had not given him a chance to sing the music he had rehearsed. Several friends later commented on how brave I was even to tackle the challenge of singing the psalm. I didn't feel brave—rash, maybe, but love makes us do rash things. This was my last chance to express my love for Annie in one of the few gifts I had been given, the gift of song.

In the second reading, Paul told the Romans, "If God is for us, who can be against us?" He goes on to assert his conviction that nothing, not even death, can separate us from God's love. I don't know if Paul got it right. I did know that death had separated me from Annie's love and her from mine. I did realize that all the love I possessed for her could not bring back Annie's crooked smile and gentle voice.

For the Gospel reading, I chose Matthew 5:1-12. If any scripture other than the Twenty-third Psalm resonates with me, it is the Beatitudes, the mission statement of the Jesus community. I have meditated and prayed these verses for more than fifty years. I am convinced that, if Jesus and the early believers got that wrong, then whatever else Jesus said is at best irrelevant and at most downright counterproductive.

As the bread and wine were being presented to Father Pooch, we sang "O God Our Help in Ages Past," affirming that, while all things pass like a dream, a power behind what we can see waits to welcome us when our time comes to go home.

As folks moved slowly up the aisle to take communion, we sang the "Prayer of St. Francis," a request to become what our Maker would have us be: instruments of peace, people who strive to love rather than hate, to pardon rather than seek vengeance, to believe despite doubts, to hope for good rather than give up on humanity, to bring the light of love and compassion rather than the darkness of bitterness and scorn.

Annie loved this prayer. So did I. The gentle poetry of *Il Poverello* masked a set of principles only a saint could hope to embrace. We tried, Annie and I and our friends. I'm afraid none of us got very close, although Annie got closer than most.

"The Lord of the Dance" concluded the service. I knew Annie loved this upbeat Shaker hymn. I also believe that, if we can't learn to dance for joy, even during pain and loss, then our alleged faith isn't worth very much, and our claim to follow the Lord of the Dance is a sham.

A celebratory meal for family and friends followed the celebratory meal Jesus is said to have shared with those closest to him.

Among the surprises and most welcome guests to join in celebrating Annie's life were Bill and Nona Flynn. They had flown in from Denver to pay their last respects. Bill, a psychiatrist and addictionologist, had both professional and personal connections with Annie. Nona is an educator and child advocate. The four of us had been friends ever since the Flynns built their home up the hill from ours, behind the tee boxes of the 16th hole of The Woods' Mountainview Golf Course.

The Flynns and the Wilsons had enjoyed many rounds of golf, many get-togethers, and lunches at each other's houses and at the Walden Pub over the years. While Annie was still working, Bill would probe her with questions of what political news she could bring home from her job in the U.S. Senate.

I sat with the Flynns, the Gepharts, and the Coopers during the luncheon. I felt safe, surrounded by caring people, although that reflected more my own painful needs than any major difference between my tablemates and the 75 or so people crowded into Lackey Hall. Every person there loved Annie. Every person there would have held out the same hand of support and caring hugs as the Flynns, the Gepharts, and the Coopers.

I have one regret concerning the memorial luncheon for Annie. I was still in such a state of shock from losing her that I forgot to say a few words or invite the guests to do the same. Knowing the kinds of friends Annie had, more than a few would have wanted to share a memory or anecdote. Knowing the kind of life Annie had led, I know many of the tales would have had us all laughing.

Bill said he would like to get together for a chat before he and Nona headed back to Denver, so we arranged to have coffee at my house the next morning. Bill showed up promptly at 10 o'clock. I handed him a mug, and we sat to talk.

I told Bill in as much detail as I could about Annie's last days and how I had handled the tragedy that had stolen my wife from me. Bill, one of the most empathetic people I have ever known, asked some questions and shared his feelings about Annie, about us as a couple, and about where my life was now headed. Then, having a plane to catch, my friend gave me a warm, brotherly hug and headed home.

As I sat and mulled over our conversation, it slowly dawned on me that that the past two hours had been a compound of friendship and professional concern on Bill's part. He was my friend. He deeply felt my pain and loss. He was a psychiatrist. He was looking for certitude that I would be OK, that I could handle the stress of a life that had been ripped in half after 43 years.

I was glad I had been fully open and honest with Bill, although it would never have entered my mind to be anything but. I knew he left content in his certitude that I would survive. He knew I was devastated by my loss. He also learned that I had somehow found the inner resources to survive and get past what had happened. I wonder what Bill would have done if he had felt less assured about whether I could cope. I'll never know, but Bill being Bill, I am certain he would have brought the full arsenal of his friendship and professional talents to bear to get me safely through the crisis if such had been necessary.

Chapter 16

Grave Stone

I had no experience to bring to the challenge of managing Annie's funeral. Initially, I didn't know who to approach to have the grave opened in the Hedges Chapel cemetery. I had to find out who would make the headstone and how to order one. Once I had gotten the name of the chapel member in charge of the cemetery, I had to wait until he located the name of the gravedigger. Then I had to catch up with the him to to request that he dig the grave. In my clueless inexperience, I had also neglected to order a headstone. I didn't even know how to order one—what kind to get, what it would cost, or how long it would take. I soon found out—with a vengeance.

We buried Annie on September 2. I phoned Misty Wall about a headstone the next week. "Go to our website, pick out the stone you want and email me the information you want to be carved on the stone," Misty told me. It seems even hardscrabble farmers in West Virginia are internet-savvy.

I did as I was told. Misty emailed me back a layout, which I approved, and we were off and running. Or so I thought.

Friends who had been down this alley told me headstones took a long time. Clueless, I accepted that information, not bothering to parse "long." October passed. November passed. December came. I called Misty, fearful that the weather would soon freeze the soil in the cemetery and make it impossible to lay the stone.

"We expect a truck Friday. They never tell me what stones they're delivering, but yours should be on the truck."

Friday came and went. The weekend passed. By Wednesday, I was beginning to panic. A week later, I called Misty again.

We would have this conversation three or four times between December and March. Each conversation was as fruitless and surreal as the initial phone call. One day in March, after a long hiatus, I managed to reach Misty. "I must have missed your call," I said, giving her the benefit of the doubt. "No, I lost my phone. It had all the numbers of our customers, so I was unable to reach you."

Maybe this was the case. Maybe she was saving face. I didn't know. Or care. I just wanted a stone on Annie's grave.

"By the way, did you send a check for half the cost of the stone when you ordered it?" Mind you, this was seven months after I had placed the original order.

"No. No one told me I had to."

"Well, the company won't start manufacturing the stone until they have half the money upfront."

On April 1—who said God doesn't have a sense of humor? —I sent Walls Monuments a check for $349.36. I hoped against hope that fronting half the money would accelerate manufacturing the gravestone I had ordered.

Silly me. Annie was dead and in the ground for more than eight months. Nothing marked where her ashes lay. In my ignorance, I didn't know that funeral directors put a small metal marker at the head of the grave to indicate where the monument goes. No such marker signaled Annie's final resting place. I panicked when this realization hit me. Suppose we put the stone over the wrong person?

No need to worry. This 160-year-old cemetery has been carefully mapped. The custodian of the plots knew exactly where Annie's ashes had been buried. My challenge was not to find her grave but to get a date when the stone would be delivered.

Spring came to the mountains. The redbuds bloomed and lapsed into their musty green summer wardrobe. The golf course opened. The pools opened. We celebrated Memorial Day, without a memorial to Annie in place. We celebrated Flag Day. In late June, Misty called. Annie would have her headstone by the end of the month.

June ended, but not my hopes for an eventual resolution of the elusive headstone affair. Finally, Misty called and said they expected to place the stone on Friday, July 3. July 4th came and went. We had beautiful fireworks at The Woods, but Annie had no headstone.

Then, on Wednesday, July 8, Misty said the stone would be in place on Thursday. Thursday came and went. No stone. Late Friday, Misty called. "What cemetery is your wife in?" Scarcely believing my ears, I mumbled, "Hedges Chapel." "No wonder we couldn't find it. We're in the cemetery at Shanghai." Shanghai is a semi-deserted farm village some 20 miles south of Hedges Chapel. "We'll place the stone tomorrow." Well, tomorrow turned out to be Saturday, July 11th, just about ten months from the day I ordered Annie's monument.

Of the two of us, I was the patient one. I make allowances for the inevitable fallibility of human nature.

Annie—punctual, detail-oriented, and faithful to commitments—became hyper-righteous when people failed to live up to their responsibilities or miss deadlines. I shuddered to think what might have happened had it been my ashes that needed a stone throughout the fall, winter, and spring of a West Virginia year.

Chapter 17

Last Blessing

The day for closure, if such a thing existed, was July 11, nearly a year after Anne's death. Her gravestone was in place and awaiting the blessing that her friend, Rev. Penny Gladwell, would bestow on this piece of gray granite.

Penny, one of the ministers who served our little community chapel, was Annie's frequent golfing companion. They had served together on several committees of The Woods Women's Golf Association. Annie, with her penchant for creative nicknames, had dubbed Penny, a United Methodist minister, "Mother Superior."

That's how Annie's "Mother Superior" and friend came to perform the service of putting the final period to the sentence of Annie's life journey. A small clutch of friends gathered around her grave. The Mountain Lake Singers offered up "Amazing Grace" one last time. I felt a sense of finality that had not characterized the other services at which we had praised God "who promised good" to us.

Penny read several brief scripture passages. Then she offered a prayer of blessing over the headstone:

"We now fondly dedicate this monument to the blessed memory of Patricia Anne Wilson, realizing that her remains lie not only in this plot of ground but in every heart her life did touch.

"We are grateful for the years we were privileged to share with Anne, years when she brought us so many pleasures and taught us so very much by example. And even though Anne has left our midst, we know she will never leave our hearts where her memory will endure as a blessing forever."

We bowed our heads as Penny read Annie's favorite poem one last time and reminded us that "Anne has fought the good fight. Anne has finished the race. Ann has kept the faith."

The service was completed; we all trooped down to the Walden Pub for a final gathering of fellowship and refreshments.

Gertie Unger, far more a friend than the woman who cleaned our house and waited tables at the pub, gave me a strong, tear-stained hug and took our orders.

As the meal wound to a conclusion, and I stood to thank my gathered friends:

"You're the people who supported me throughout this awful time," I said, or words to that effect. I thanked Ann Gephart for so generously driving me to visit Annie in Morgantown and for wandering about the city and dealing with the Hastings Funeral Home. I thanked my friend Ron, Ann's husband, who was battling radiation treatments after surgery for throat cancer, for tolerating my need to preempt so much of his wife's time during the weeks following Annie's accident.

I thanked the Ramseths for stepping in to care for the pets when Annie's crisis necessitated so much absence so I could be with her at the hospital.

I looked down at Dave Cooper, my fellow Mountain Lake Singer, and his wife Vicki, our unofficial manager and den mother. I thanked Dave, Lee, and Kat for being so generous with their time and talent, for joining me to celebrate her life with their gift of song and for showing up virtually every Thursday following Annie's funeral to practice our music.

I looked at Dave again and almost choked with tears of gratitude. "You knew I had to sing, didn't you? You knew I had to be able to get through 'Annie's Song,' because of who she was and what the song said, didn't you?"

I had to pause as tears choked my voice. Dave grabbed me by the arm and whispered, "You know we love you, Bill. It was important to be with you."

Then I looked at Vicki, sitting next to Dave. "I think 'your fine Italian hand' was behind all of this, wasn't it, Vicki? You knew how necessary it was to keep me from isolating and wallowing in self-pity." Vicki didn't say a word, but her knowing smile told me that I had nailed it.

She and my fellow singers and the thirty or so people there for a farewell party for Annie had succeeded in doing for me what I surely could not have done for myself. They had lifted me up. They had been my strength. They had pulled me into life when I wanted to run and hide. I'd like to think they did it because I deserved such love and friendship. My heart told me that caring for me, loving me when I could scarcely love myself, was simply another way these good people loved Annie. They were repaying, through kindness and caring, the love and friendship Annie had bounteously spent throughout her life on anybody who crossed her path.

Once again, I had benefited from her generosity. Annie had sown, and I was reaping the harvest of love and friendship that she had planted.

Chapter 18

Moving On

I'm not sure I believe in premonitions. However, I know people who claim awareness of future events, and I think Shakespeare got it right when he has Hamlet tell his pal: "There are more things in heaven and earth, Horatio, than are dreamt of in your philosophy."

Maybe Annie had a premonition; maybe she didn't. In the last year or so of her life, she would frequently tell folks: "If I die before Bill, he'll move to Auburn to be near Claire."

Naturally, I took umbrage at this prognostication. I reminded Annie that the actuarial tables were stacked in favor of women outliving men. I chided her for thinking she knew what decision I should make about where to move in the high improbability that I outlived her.

But then, Annie did have control issues, inherited from her black-belt controlling mother. She certainly did claim priority in which way decisions went in our family. And, most likely, she knew me better than I knew myself. Within 15 months of her death, I had moved to Auburn, Alabama, to be near my daughter Claire and her family.

I planned the move almost as soon as we had blessed Annie's grave marker. Our 3,200 square-foot house had way more space than I needed. The expense and effort required to maintain this residence and its half-acre lot would be a serious drain on the single income that would now finance my lifestyle.

As much as I cherished my friends of many years at The Woods, when the time came to deal with my rapidly approaching old age, I knew that family would of necessity come first. Finally, every item in the house, every room, every view evoked memories of Annie. Most were happy and good. Even so, I knew that constantly living in the shadow of our 43-years together would not be a good thing. My emotional recovery demanded that I git while the gittin' was good. And, once again, dammit, Annie had proven to be smarter than I.

The house went on the market in the fall of 2015. The following October, I had an offer too good to refuse. The catch was—there is always a catch! —that I had to vacate the house in a month. My buyers had sold their house in nearby Charles Town. They had to be out, so I had to be out.

Like most of the curve balls life throws at us, the compressed timetable turned out to be a blessing in disguise. Annie didn't call me "Mr. Mañana" for nothing. If I had been given six months to move, I would have used all 180 days to complete my relocation. As it was, a 30-day deadline forced me to deal with things I would just as soon have ignored.

One more time, the many friends Annie and I had made proved to be a lifesaver. I hate to ask for help. But old friends have the franchise to know what you need and when to tell you that you need to accept their offer of help. Half a dozen folks trooped into the house, surrounded by cartons, packing tape, wrapping paper, and labels. They ganged up on me and on 28 years' worth of stuff.

Ann Gephart and Jackie Wolfe tackled the kitchen, always alien turf to me. They packed glasses, dishes, pots, pans, and flatware. These two friends knew better than I what a guy would need when he moved into a two-bedroom apartment measuring about 800 square feet. They unsentimentally packed everything into cartons. A relatively small number of boxes was for my move. Many others went into my friend Bob Selepak's truck to be hauled to Goodwill. Other cases went into the Gepharts' garage for the Woods Yard Sale the following spring. Some got trashed.

Vicki and Kat Cooper tackled the bedroom's walk-in closet: linens, towels, any of Annie's clothes that had not already been donated to a local church, my surplus clothes, and a bunch of stuff in various places in the master bathroom that defied any organizational thoughts I might have harbored.

"Are you sure you can do this?" I innocently asked Vicki.

"I'm a military wife," she shot back. "Dave spent 25 years in the Coast Guard. I moved 20 times. I can do this."

Then, with all the tact of a marine drill sergeant, Vicki told me of her 20-second rule. "You get 20 seconds to decide," she warned. "Keep it. Donate it. Discard it. What you don't keep or give away in those 20 seconds gets trashed." I soon found out she wasn't kidding,

There's a huge nostalgia in having to deal with more than 25 years of your life. Memories crowd in. Some things evoke a smile. Some tear the scab off a long-forgotten sorrow or regret. Regardless, to create a future, the past must either be integrated or laid to rest. My dear friends were doing that job for me. In my ongoing emotional and mental numbness, I had become teachable, docile. Down the road, I might have resisted, dug in my heels. Still in the throes of my loss, I obediently followed their lead toward my new life.

The day came. Packing, donating, and discarding were over. Boxes filled just about every room in the house. The movers showed up—three Croatians, young, strong, tough. These guys looked more like they should be toting AK-47s in the hills of Yugoslavia rather than going through roll after roll of packing tape.

My friends and I—mostly them—had secured the safe stuff and a few valuables I would carry with me to Alabama. The Croats packed all the furniture destined for my new apartment, plus two armoires full of crystal, china, and porcelain figurines. Annie's prized curio collection was now part of her legacy to Claire.

Annie and I had shared the last 14 years with three pets, two dogs, and a calico cat. The 15 months following Annie's death had not been particularly kind to me or the dogs. Gus and Sadie, my Bichon Frises, were siblings—same parents, different litters. They shared the same DNA. Neither lived to make the move to Auburn.

As Gus approached his 15th birthday in December of 2015, he developed incurable kidney disease. He had to be euthanized. All my grief was still focused on Annie. So, poor Gus never got the mourning he deserved.

Ten months later, Sadie crossed the Rainbow Bridge. She, too, was hit by incurable kidney disease. Euthanized less than a week after being diagnosed, Sweet Sadie, as I thought of her, did get mourned, did break my heart. Beloved four-legged companions will do that every time.

The fully loaded truck rumbled down my curved driveway without taking out any trees. That left Molly and me and a Chrysler van full of stuff too personal or precious to be trusted to the moving company. Molly, always a good traveler, went somewhat reluctantly into her carrying case. She seemed almost aware that this was her last goodbye to the only home she had ever known.

Bungee cords secured her purple crate on the console between the front seats of the van, and I headed east on WV Rt. 9 into Martinsburg. One last time, I passed the site of Annie's fatal accident by the Tomahawk Middle School. At least, I thought, I won't be reminded of the accident every time I drive into town. At the law office of Stephen R. Kirshner, I signed the papers that put closure to a quarter-century of my life and to the longest, most loving relationship I had ever known. Then I turned around and drove the two blocks west to I-81 southbound.

The future, whatever it might be, lay 700-plus miles away. No one, particularly me, had any idea what awaited me in Auburn, Alabama.

Chapter 19

Just Molly and Me

I had driven I-81 south so often when Annie and I wintered in Florida that if the Chrysler van had been a horse, I could have given the critter its head and slept the entire trip. The drive had become almost boring enough to make it unsafe.

Molly and I headed for Knoxville, Tennessee, 454 miles to the southwest, the longest leg of our two-day trip.

Molly, a seasoned traveler, let out an occasional soft "meow" to remind me that she would like a kibble treat. That given, Molly and I settled back into our quiet routine, accompanied by the strains of Mozart on SiriusXM radio.

What a gift Sirius is. Gone are the days when 100 miles south of Winchester, one faced an unending torrent of Bible-Belt preaching and country music. Now, one can venture through the Blue Ridge and Piedmont to the strains of Vivaldi, the pounding rhythms of Chuck Berry, or the syrup on pancakes of Willy Nelson's West Texas drawl.

Loading the van and signing off on the sale had taken most of the morning, so the sun was setting by the time my Town & Country rolled into the parking lot of the Knoxville LaQuinta Inn. LaQuinta had been our home on the road ever since I learned that pets were welcome at no extra charge. The accommodations were clean, in this case, almost brand new, and perfectly adequate for a one-night stay.

Molly liked LaQuinta because there were plenty of hiding spaces, making every morning's effort to return her to the purple carrying case an even greater challenge. More than once, I had been forced to pull my Callaway driver out of the golf bag to serve as a prod to dislodge Miss Molly from a corner behind the headboard. I figured that after a certain time playing "catch me if you can," she was lucky I hadn't brained her with the golf club.

Morning came. I packed our bags and loaded them onto the brass trolley all hotels supply to heavily laden guests. Molly and I headed down the hall toward the car to resume our journey south. Her purple case was perched safely, I thought, on the front of the trolley. I didn't put any bags on top of or in front of the case since this might scare the poor feline.

Well, Molly got the fright of her life anyway. The trolley hit a bump. Molly's case executed a perfect front somersault that would have been worth 10 points in a gymnastics competition. She didn't appreciate the execution or the potential score. Rather I heard a squeal and scrambling from the catapulted calico.

With the case back on the trolley, this time even farther back from the front edge and sitting squarely on the flat surface of the conveyance, Molly and I headed back down the hallway. I was extra cautious, realizing that the tumble had been far more traumatic for the cat than for me.

Whoops! Another bump. Another somersault. Another groan, louder this time, and another frantic scrambling from the upended critter. Even I was upset by the turn of events. But with no alternative except to keep on truckin', I made it to the van, secured Molly's case with bungee cords, bribed her with some treats, and hit the road.

A few miles along the way to Chattanooga, I noted that Molly, in a huge fit of pique, had refused to even touch her favorite kitty snacks. Talk about passive-aggressive behavior! We rode in silence. Molly out of resentment and distress. Me out of my inability to speak cat.

For me, the odd thing about this 317-mile drive was that Molly, who is usually a rather verbal kitty, remained mum. If her traumatic tumble had not damaged her ego, it had affected her vocal cords.

The van headed relentlessly south through the hills of northwest Alabama. Gadsden and Anniston flew by. I managed to elude the turn-off for Birmingham—a nice enough city, but not on my relocation itinerary. By mid-afternoon, I pulled into the Villages at Lakeside, my new home and Molly's, hooked up with Claire and began unloading the Town and Country.

I liberated Molly first, in a guilt-ridden act of amends. The traumatized cat scooted under my brand-new bed, not to surface for the next 24 hours. If she snuck out that evening for a drink of water, I never heard her. She certainly showed no inclination for most of the first week to forgive and forget.

For better or for worse, my cat and I had found our new home and moved in. I was as clueless as Molly as to what the future would hold. Like her, I was hoping mightily that life would not dump me on my head anytime in the near future.

Chapter 20

Sweet Home Alabama

Robert Frost may have said it best: "Home is the place where, when you go there, they have to take you in." Molly and I were about to find that out for ourselves. Cats don't do much self-reflection as far as I can tell. I do. So, during the drive south from Knoxville, as the big grey-blue van lumbered into the Villages at Lakeside, I couldn't help but wonder what my future would become, who I would become.

Bereft of the woman I had loved and who had loved me for more than half my life, what was left? What could I, should I, care about? I could mark time until I ran out of it. I could chase new experiences like a kid in a toy store. After all, Auburn might be a new toy store for me. Maybe it would be a happy place, a place where I could learn to play again.

Unpacking, dealing with the Croatians unloading my stuff, stowing seven furniture pads they had forgotten or deliberately abandoned, precluded much thinking initially. Claire and granddaughter Lucy were the catalysts on the arrival end. They relentlessly unpacked what was left of the stuff of my life, just as Ann Gephart, Jackie Wolfe, Vicki, and Kat Cooper, and a battalion of friends had eased my way out of my West Virginia home of 27 years.

Lucy, bless her heart, said, "I love to hang pictures." Tack hammer and brads in hand, she proceeded to do so with a flair I could not muster. What I would have dawdled over for weeks, she finished in a matter of days.

Frost was right: I got to Auburn, and they took me in. Molly and I had a new home, although it took her almost a week to get over her dumpings in Knoxville. I had a family: Claire and Jon, who is like the son I never had. Lucy and Mary, the granddaughters I cherished but whom geography and the living of their lives had made all too scarce in my life. Amidst the wreckage of my now-widowed life, one positive emerged: I could be a dad and an admiring friend to my daughter and son-in-law, and a doting grandfather to the Bolton girls.

Out of concern to ease my transition, Claire had assembled several things I needed to do, groups I needed to join.

There was the Lee County Historical Society. As a non-historian with only an amateur's interest in the past, I felt little attraction to the mandate of the group. But it did afford me a place to go. It opened up opportunities to meet friendly people, many of whom knew Claire because of her job as senior editor of the online Encyclopedia of Alabama.

Claire urged me to join the Jule Collins Smith Museum of Fine Art and the Chamber Music Society it housed. More to do, more to meet. More people willing, in their charming southern hospitality, to extend the hand of friendship. I demurred at signing up for the Opelika-based Arts Association of East Alabama, although I did add my name to their roster and have attended a few events—concerts and musical theatre.

My darling daughter, it seemed, had decided to get the old man from the mountains of West Virginia inserted into the culture of a quasi-sleepy southern college town. I later asked Claire why she didn't join the Chamber Music Society or the Arts Association. "I don't like classical music or musical theater." I never again invited Claire or Jon to a local cultural happening.

We did share one interest that continues to enrich my life on almost a weekly basis: The Red Clay Brewery, twenty minutes away in Opelika, hosts Irish music sessions every Wednesday evening. I had been a few times on flying visits to Auburn. Now the sessions are a highlight of my week. Several of the musicians have extended the hand of friendship. They have also politely and accurately told me that my level of guitar strumming would not qualify me for admission to the band.

For the record, a session to the Irish is not a concert. You go to a "concert" to watch and listen. You may clap or tap your feet to the jigs and reels, but you are expected to be quiet and courteous when the musicians are doing their thing.

A "session" is to a concert as a rock concert is to Philharmonic Hall. The band plays on. Who and how many musicians join in on any given Wednesday depends mostly on who walks through the brew pub's door and what instrument he or she may bring. The audience, a misnomer if ever there was one, quaffs a microbrew of their choosing from the list of 20 or so featured that evening on the chalkboard behind the bar. A non-drinker, I nurse a can of Coke, the only alcohol-free product dispensed by the barkeep.

Irish music night has enriched my experience of Alabama and led to unforeseen, happy changes. Douglas Coutts is a retired diplomat, expert on world hunger, and adroit player of Irish rhythms. He also took on the role of a mentor to me as I transitioned into life at Auburn.

"You need to join OLLI," he told me the first time we met. (For a Canadian, Doug is not long on circumlocution.)

"Why? What is OLLI?" said I, thinking of the pal of Kukla and Fran in black and white TV days.

"Because you can take interesting courses and meet interesting people. OLLI is a sort of adult education for old folks. Most of the presenters are retired professors or teachers who want to stay active and want to share their knowledge with their peers." Being willing to have Doug play Virgil to my Dante, I signed up for a poetry writing class in the winter semester of OLLI. I also joined a drawing seminar and a reading/discussion group.

I have become, at least in my mind, a minor poet as a result of the interest shown by Ken Autrey, a real poet and facile teacher. I still can't draw, so I will pass over my encounter with charcoal and No. 2 pencils in silence. The reading/discussion led by Ed Hornig, a retired Lutheran pastor, changed my life, radically and for the better.

In the closing minutes of Ed's final class, I sat placidly in the last row on the right side of an open rectangle, Ed's usual layout for his discussion group. The chair to my right was empty until an attractive woman of a certain age quietly settled into it.

As the class ended, Ed walked back to our table and pointed to me and the woman next to me.

"You two need to get together."

"Why?"

"Because she lost her husband a month after you lost your wife."

Since I was well into the first draft of a book on becoming a widower—this book—I introduced myself to my neighbor. I learned her name and that her husband, a retired professor, had died suddenly of a massive coronary in September 2015. I handed her my card and said:

"Would you like to have coffee so we can talk about our loss? Maybe I can learn from your experience as I write my book."

She wisely demurred and commented that she didn't have a card to give me her number. I said that was fine.

"If you want to have coffee to discuss your loss, just give me a call."

Class ended, and we went our separate ways. This charming woman, however, had piqued my interest, although my focus was still to obtain any insights she might care to impart about dealing with the loss of a spouse.

Mentally and emotionally, I was still benumbed at the loss of Annie 20 months previously. I was not looking for a lady friend, much less a dating relationship, whatever that means at the ripe age of 81.

For several days I waited in vain for a call. Had I come on too strong? Did the lady suspect a nonexistent ulterior motive? Had I come on too mildly? Did I give the impression that I didn't care whether she called or not?

Then the phone rang. It was my erstwhile classmate. By that time, Claire and Jon had introduced me to Amsterdam Cafe, one of the nicer eateries in Auburn. Since I love to eat out and because I felt I owed this kind lady more than a cup of coffee for her insights into widowhood, I said, "Would you like to have lunch at Amsterdam?" Little did I know what I later found out: Amsterdam was also one of her favorite restaurants. In my ignorance, I had hit a home run.

We met at Amsterdam on May 10. This retired art historian/teacher turned out to be a fascinating lunch companion. That I was an actual writer somehow intrigued her. We did very little talking about our respective losses, but we did sense in each other a depth of sorrow and pain that enhanced our ability to get beyond the usual "chitchat" of a first dining experience.

Rather quickly, we began seeing each other regularly. Eventually, we did end up sharing our grief journeys—and much more. We are still sharing and learning to appreciate that catastrophic grief does not mean one's life has to come to a halt.

There is life after loss. There is love after sorrow. As Orphan Annie so well put it, "The sun will be up tomorrow." That's true even when you think there is nothing but dark sadness in your future.

PART 2—The Road Map

What I Learned

Chapter 21

Welcome to the Club

The reality is that you will grieve forever. You will not 'get over' the loss of a loved one; you will learn to live with it. You will heal, and you will rebuild yourself around the loss you have suffered. You will be whole again, but you will never be the same. Nor should you be the same, nor would you want to.
    Elisabeth Kübler-Ross and John Kessler
    (www.cragman.com)

Annie's death automatically made me a member of an exclusive club that nobody wants to join: the 800,000 Americans who lose spouses each year. The grim prediction of how grief unfolds by Kubler-Ross and Kessler offers no joy, but it does frame a reasonably accurate description of my life since Annie left me.

I have mourned. I have not ceased to mourn. I have accepted a painful reality that I cannot change. Healing has set in with the help of another widowed person who walks the same path. I'm whole yet, but I am more complete than I have been since August 24, 2015. I do not wish to relive the past. But I am not, nor will I ever be, the same.

I had to face some challenging questions as I started to tell my sad tale: How do you write a memoir? How do you write the story of soul-crushing grief? How do you describe becoming a half where you used to be a whole? When I started, I had no idea of my destination. I had never been down this road. First, I tried writing a survival manual, a "how-to" book called *Beware of Widows Bearing Casseroles*. After four and a half chapters, I ran out of gas. Maybe I didn't run out of gas. Maybe I ran out of motivation. Or need.

I didn't know it then, but that first attempt served as therapy for me. I needed a way to cope with losing the love of my life. I talked myself into thinking that a book for men who grieved like me would be a fine thing, especially if I could keep it light-hearted. Eventually, I learned that you cannot do "lighthearted" with a broken heart. My original effort held no answers, so I stopped trying.

The present book attempts to give my fellow club members a modicum of hope by laying out my story. If I can show how I got through this, maybe they can emerge from their grief, too.

I have no other experience of being widowed than this one. The only gift I can offer to anyone looking for solace during a soul-crushing loss is to say, "Welcome. Others truly do share your grief, feel your pain. I am one of them."

Chapter 22

I Was Not Alone

I learned that as a widower, I have lots of company. The U.S. Census Bureau reports that in 2016 widows accounted for 34% of older women. There were more than three times as many widows (8.8 million) as widowers (2.6 million). [*A Profile of Older Americans:2016*, Administration on Aging, Administration for Community Living, U.S. Department of Health and Human Services, p. 4.]

Widows outnumber men, and by an increasing margin: 34% of women 65 or older are widows; 12% of men 65 and older are widowers. As we age, the numbers grow, and the statistical gap widens: 73% of women 85 or older are widows. 34% of men 85 or older are widowers. [*2016. Older Americans: Key Indicators of Well-Being*, Federal Interagency Forum on Aging-Related Statistics, p. 5.]

Women outnumber men, and increasingly so, as we age. In 2014, women accounted for 56% of the population age 65 and older. They accounted for 66% of the population 85 and over. [Ibid., p. 3.] For men seeking remarriage, the talent pool may be larger, but it is also shallower: Only 2% of older widows want to remarry, but 20% of older men want to tie the knot again.

Some, but not all of us, remarry. When Annie died, I didn't even think about marriage. I wasn't even ready to try to figure out how to date! For many of the widowed, remarriage also involves economics.

My wife worked for the government. I still receive part of her annuity. Her federal health insurance has passed to me. If I remarry, those two benefits disappear. These facts have an extremely chilling effect on prospects for remarriage.

That said, the lawyer who redid my will after I lost my wife would probably disagree. She said, almost apologetically, "I hate to tell you this, Mr. Wilson, but my experience is that most men remarry rather quickly after they lose their wives. They can't stand the loneliness."

The Census Bureau agrees. On average, widowers will remarry within three years. Widows, within five years. Census Bureau data are probably low. A number of those who have lost spouses don't show up in the statistics. They simply get remarried and move on.

Why do widowers remarry?

For all kinds of reasons:

Loneliness. I was blessed. I had found the right partner. I got comfortable in my marriage. Most men do, to some extent.

Our spouse becomes as comfortable as the old sweater or the tattered sneakers we love to hang out in. Take away the wife, and the parts don't fit together. There aren't enough parts. Death has shattered the whole. Half a marriage is no marriage at all. That certainly was my experience.

Social ineptitude. My wife was the catalyst in our social life. My extroverted spouse nurtured old friendships and built new ones; she kept the social calendar—meticulously. She wouldn't even let me touch it or make a social commitment—for good reasons. I usually got the wrong date, the wrong day, the wrong time, the wrong people. Once, I even got the wrong month!

Annie was a gracious, welcoming hostess to anyone who came within a hundred yards of our house. When she left, my social skills went with her. So did any hope I had of successfully entertaining friends and neighbors.

Domestic ineptitude. Some guys cook. I don't. If Campbell didn't make "Hearty Soups" and Publix didn't make good subs, I might starve or go broke paying restaurant tabs. I can cook if you put a gun to my head. Otherwise, my preferred domestic tool is the microwave. I can clean as well as anybody, but being congenitally lazy, I'll hire a cleaning lady until the money runs out.

Life management skills. Men, at least this man, don't cope too well with the stuff of life in half a partnership. I can manage—barely. I greatly preferred to let my wife do the heavy lifting in our social and domestic life. When she made it clear that I had to step up to bat, most of the time I did. Sometimes, even willingly.

My chronic cluelessness to the commonly accepted signals that the time had arrived to do something—anything— meant that I needed Annie to remind me to put up or take down the Christmas tree, to create a birthday card for one of our nieces, or to fix a toilet that was no longer capable of shutting off automatically.

Home maintenance skills. I have watched widowed friends struggle with all the consequences of losing a partner. Most manage pretty well. Several women I know have mastered the basic "guy" stuff: minor repairs, yard work, dealing with financial and legal matters.

When it comes to the flip side of that equation, men—certainly this man—are a distant second. We don't do too well cooking, cleaning, dusting, folding laundry, shopping, planning social events, remembering birthdays, etc. I know only one guy who knows how to iron a shirt—and he is not even a widower. He just irons better than his wife. And bakes better than her, too.

Chapter 23

I Was Not Unique

Death sucks. Grief stinks. No one wants to die. No one wants to mourn the dead. Sooner or later, however, we all lose loved ones, unless death grabs us. Then, our mourning problem is solved. Well, it just becomes someone else's problem.

A widowed friend of mine once told me: Every marriage, every committed relationship ends badly. Divorce ruptures some. Death terminates others. No exceptions. No gentle letdowns. At some point, we all end up alone, or we just plain end up, leaving someone else alone.

Numb, baffled by Annie's death, I felt like I had just been transported to the Land of the Lost. Supportive family, friends, and a particularly empathetic shock-trauma surgeon enabled me to do what was needed. The foresight both Annie and I had taken to discuss our last wishes and to prepare the necessary legal documents took away any guilt feelings over the painful choice I made on my wife's behalf. She would have done the same for me.

Even though Annie's death came as a total surprise, I was no stranger to grief. I had mourned loved ones before:

- My dad dropped dead of a heart attack during my senior year of college.
- My mom died some 20 years after my dad, 72 hours after suffering a massive brain stem stroke.
- My first wife and I had two miscarriages. We had no decision to make, no anticipation of what happened. We just lost two babies. It broke our hearts. Eventually, it contributed to breaking our marriage.
- My second daughter died of pneumonia at age 40. No one expected it—not her mom, not my second wife nor I, not her big sister, and certainly not my daughter, who lay down for a nap and never got up.
- My older sister died of bone cancer at age 84.

What's the point of this morbid litany? None of us is unique. People die. We die. People grieve. We grieve for them, or they grieve for us. The Grim Reaper is an equal-opportunity destroyer. I will die. I have grieved more than once for someone else. That's life. As Jim Morrison said, "No one here gets out alive."

So, should we just suck it up and soldier bravely through the loss? Hell no! Longfellow said: "Life is real! Life is earnest! And the grave is not its goal; Dust thou art, to dust returnest, Was not spoken of the soul."

I'm not sure about Longfellow's take on the soul. That's a conundrum each of us must solve for ourselves. I do know from personal experience that, if life is real, death is a hell of a lot more real! We may be able to live a life of denial and self-delusion, but we can't escape or deny death, our own or that of others. Death happens. Inevitably. Unavoidably. Undeniably.

When Annie's heart stopped, I was immersed in an experience that is common to humankind. But I didn't feel that way. I didn't think that way. I felt unique—probably because I felt alone.

Reminded of the old black-and-white Tarzan movies, I felt as if I were standing by myself, isolated and alone, in the elephants' graveyard. Grayness and bleakness surrounded me. Stuck in a morass where nothing would ever change, I would find no joy. The sun would never shine. The mists of mourning would waft around my ankles forever. I had no clue what to do or where to go to escape this barren place.

I did not know that time and persistence might ease my pain, that trial and error, taking the next step, doing the next dumb thing might eventually lead me to a better place. I didn't know or care that there might even be a better place toward which I might move.

We die alone. Grief steals our hope. Mourning is a painful, erratic journey at best. And I found myself, as all mourners do, at the start of a process that had no clear-cut end, no certain direction, no predictable timetable. The word that best described my situation was godforsaken. Widowhood is a terrible place. If this is a journey, I have yet to find the road map.

Chapter 24

I Was Not All That Different

With so many differences between men and women, mostly weighted in favor of widows, do we have anything in common? More than you might think. Consider:

When a spouse dies, suddenly or after a long illness, we have lost a major part of our life—a key, unique relationship. Worst case, let's say you hated your wife. She still formed one of the main focal points of your day. At a minimum, you had to figure out how to avoid her, how to avoid offending her, how to cope with her tantrums when you did make her angry, how to keep pouring oil on the troubled waters of your marriage.

Depending on your ethical code, you might invest a lot of energy figuring out how to get a little something on the side without getting caught. All of those complications go down the drain when your spouse dies. The question that looms large is: "What do I do next?"

When you lose a mate, something is missing. You need to figure out what that is and how to deal with it.

I had the other kind of marriage. I loved my wife. When she died, I had nothing to love but her memory. Should I run right out to find someone else to love? I had already tried that quick fix shortly before I met Annie when a relationship ended. At least for me, love on the rebound didn't work.

After I emerged from what can only be described as a mad, passionate love affair blew up after three weeks, Annie came along. My new "girlfriend" and I wisely spent two years getting to know each other—actually living together—before deciding to marry. You see, we had both survived first marriages that hadn't worked out so well. We were a bit gun-shy about taking the plunge again.

Long story short, we must have gotten something right. The marriage lasted for forty-one years. We still loved and liked each other the day she walked out the door never to return! Good for the marriage. Good for us as a couple committed to each other. Bad for me when I lost Annie.

Based on my experience and scores of firsthand accounts by others, the above statements summarize how the typical grief journey progresses if there even is such a thing as typical. I did not choose my grief journey. It chose me.

I also learned that my grief may be special, but I'm not. Lots of people lose spouses. Most recover, but we aren't cured. Nobody gets cured. There is no cure. Given a choice between "Time heals all wounds" and memoirist Frank Case's "Time wounds all heels," I'd put my money on Case.

Chapter 25

But My Grief Was All Mine

We who mourn our dead are not unique. Grief appeared the first time a protohuman lost a parent, child, or mate. Mourning will not cease until the penultimate human being stands alone on a dying planet after his or her mate, child or parent has succumbed to whatever will make the human race extinct.

Do we despair then? Since we're all in the same boat, do death and mourning even merit the emotional energy we invest in them?

I thought about the points Doctor Kübler-Ross was making:

- My grief was permanent;
- My grief was mine, no one else's;
- My grief would not just go away;
- I would most likely survive;
- But I would not forget;
- The death of a loved one would change me, permanently;
- I would probably incorporate my loss into who I am and move on;
- No one has the right to tell me how, how long, or how deeply to mourn my loss.

Grief is permanent. Annie passed over to wherever we go if we go anywhere. Her death terminated 43 years of two lives being intertwined. My sense of bonding, of shared feelings, of experiences remembered didn't disappear just because Annie did. After an amputation, the phantom pain remains. Ripping a scab off a wound doesn't heal it. We can turn off a shrill car alarm, but the sound will resonate in our brains, often for hours.

My grief was mine, no one else's. Friends, family and acquaintances occasionally said they knew how I felt. They didn't. They will never know, even after they lose one of their own loved ones. My loss—anyone's loss—of a loved person (or pet) ends a unique relationship. No two creatures on the planet are the same—not identical twins, not littermates, not clones. Annie's death shattered a bond like no other.

I had lost a spouse; no living member of my family or Annie's knew what that death cost me, just as no one in either family knew what went on—good or bad—behind closed doors. The same holds for all of us. Friends will empathize. Out of their love, they will try to assuage our grief. They will fail. Also, as time passes, they will get on with their lives and we will gradually fall off their radar.

Those who mishandle the situation with ill-advised comments or advice will do more than fail. They will make things worse. No one needs to hear, "God wanted another angel." No one should be told, "You've mourned him or her long enough. It's time to start dating." It is wrong to say, "You should get another dog (cat, parakeet) right away." Walk a mile in my shoes may be good advice. Those seeking to comfort the sorrowful will never succeed in this challenge.

Grief does not just go away. Things would be great if it did. I loved and lost someone. I could not find a quick fix. I discovered slowly and painfully that time alone would not heal my wounds. It lessened the pain. It created room for new experiences, a new life, even new love. But the loss endures.

Our experiences make us who we are. Conscious or not, what we have done, whom we have known, the things we have learned are part of our makeup. Death does not erase them.

Psychiatrists, psychologists, and counselors spend hours helping us deal with the memories that reveal who and what has shaped us. I had lived long enough to know that I could not drown the past in frantic activities, substitute hobbies for the pain of aloneness, or rush into a relationship so that someone new could "fix" me. Marcel Proust wasn't the only writer to expound on how things past influence our present. Each of us is a work in progress. We don't get to choose the raw material that nature and nurture dump in our laps.

I felt my life was over when Annie died, but the fact is, I survived. When some couples have been together for a long, long time, one sometimes dies within hours or weeks of the other. Obviously, that was not my situation.

Occasionally, a grief-stricken spouse commits suicide because he or she cannot handle being left behind. But not I. Like most folks, I got out of bed the morning after I buried Annie and got on with life. I didn't want to. I had no desire to get back on the horse. But I did. I didn't see any alternative.

Annie died. I still had to feed and walk my dogs. I had to feed the cat and clean her litter box. Life had a nasty way of impinging on my desire to stop the world and get off.

I did not forget. My friend Urban Toucher lost his wife suddenly. Ginger died of a stroke on the operating table right after a successful cardiac procedure. She exemplified the sick joke, "The operation was a success, but the patient died."

I spoke to Urban shortly after Annie's funeral. I hoped he might have some words of wisdom to share, some comfort to offer.

"Bill," he said, "a friend of mine called me a couple of weeks ago. She had recently lost her husband and wanted to know if it ever gets easy.

"Charlotte," I told her, "it gets easier, but it never gets easy."

Annie's death has changed me permanently. As a newly single man, I found that relationships and activities based on being part of a couple gradually faded. In my new relationship, I have established new bonds; new leisure pastimes have emerged based on the interests I share with my new partner.

Annie and I played golf and bridge--partly so we could spend time together, partly because she enjoyed both activities and I enjoyed the time spent doing almost anything with her. I have not played bridge since her death. I have played golf less than a dozen times since. My new partner does not enjoy either activity. Do I miss them? No. I enjoy pastimes the new relationship has brought into my life.

I have begun to incorporate my loss into who I am and to move on. I don't miss golf. I don't miss bridge. I do miss Annie. I do enjoy learning about art from my new companion, an artist and art historian. I do enjoy writing poetry as part of a poetry salon into which I have been generously accepted. I do enjoy participating in the local Chamber Music Society. I still miss Annie and think about her often, every day. I have moved on. I have also changed. But I have not stopped being me.

I learned that no one has the right to tell me how, how long or how deeply to mourn my loss. Fortunately, no one told me to stop grieving for Annie, to stop being such a sad ass. I learned that each of us has the right to find our own path as we recover from our loss. Anyone else, no matter how well-intentioned, is a trespasser.

Chapter 26

Things I Had to learn

Grieving is a process, not an event. My wife died; I was sad. I got over it. Would that my grief journey had been that simple!

My wife died. I was devastated. Two years later, I was still grieving—but not as much, not in the same way. The feelings, the sense of loss had become less gut-wrenching. I still missed—still do miss— Annie. Often, I find myself getting ready to tell her something or suggest a TV show or invite her out to dinner only to realize she is no longer with me.

Grieving differs for each of us. My grief went by fits and starts. Widowed friends, both men, and women tell me that's also how they grieve. We each progress at our own pace, in our own way. Eventually, most of us come to a realistic acceptance that we are ready to move on. But each of us reaches this conclusion at different points in our history. If there is a finish line for the grief journey—and I'm not so sure there is—we don't all cross it at the same time.

My grief had no fixed stages. Some grief counselors try to shoehorn our journey into Dr. Kübler-Ross's five stages of death and dying as a template for grieving: denial, anger, bargaining, depression, and acceptance. This would make a nice neat package. Too bad it didn't fit me. If someone tries to fit you into this emotional straightjacket, pay no attention. Grief is not one-size-fits-all.

Many professionals claim that this template doesn't apply at all to grief. We widowers bounce around from one emotion to the next: anger, sadness, sorrow, resentment, fear, loneliness, confusion, depression. A roller-coaster ride better describes my period of mourning. There was no knowing when the next bump, turn, or vertical drop might occur.

Just as grieving is not lockstep, neither does it have any fixed endpoint. I did not get stuck in the dismal swamp of complicated grief. I slowly began to come out the other end of this horrific process. But there was no way I could anticipate an end date on my inner calendar or even know when I had reached the desired goal.

People misunderstood me. We all misunderstand those who grieve. Some folks, friends, and relatives think we are taking way too long to "get over it." Others will judge us for not being miserable enough. Some friends, and maybe the women with whom we try to reenter the dating world, will think losing a wife has made us a saint. Let's face it—if anybody was a bastard before his wife died, he will be a bastard after he loses her. An abusive drunk during a marriage will be an abusive drunk as a widower. Devastating loss does not automatically change any of us into saints.

I misunderstood others. Reentry is just as perilous for widowers as it is for astronauts. We can all too easily crash and burn. Casserole Crusaders do exist. Predation and compassion can look the same. I learned that because a widow, single woman, or divorcee was kind didn't mean she wanted to get into my pants or let me into hers. Easy does it. Let things evolve at their own pace. A wise friend gave me that advice. It proved invaluable.

I needed to learn new social skills. My wife largely constructed our social network. Annie went away, and so did a big chunk of our relations with friends. That seems almost universally inevitable. I eventually realized that I had not caused this tectonic shift in friendships. I most likely didn't do much to develop them in the first place. I did little to construct the group of pals my wife and I hung out with, played cards with, and dined out with. I have worked hard to preserve the pieces of this network I wanted to keep. Sometimes I have succeeded.

I needed to develop new domestic skills or substitutes for them. I am no Chef Boyardee or Mr. Clean. I don't do laundry or windows. I had to find surrogates. Some widowed friends have located services that deliver prepackaged foods with detailed preparation instructions. Some have joined social clubs—Elks, Moose, Knights of Columbus, VFW. They can and do find friends in these clubhouses.

I hired a cleaning service to do my house. My neighborhood has several dry cleaners and laundries. Some of them will pick up, service, and return my linens and clothes. I don't have to starve. I don't have to turn my tighty whities inside out every other day. I did have to identify and utilize those services. With no Annie to remind me, I did have to remember to pick up the dry cleaning.

To date or not to date scared me. I like women. I like women so much I married two of them (not simultaneously!). As the pain of losing Annie eased, I developed friendships with several women.

I joined an organization where I could find both women and men in my peer group who shared the same interests, did the same kinds of things, and, in at least some instances, had also lost spouses.

But I hadn't dated anyone other than Annie in 43 years. I didn't know how to ask a woman on a date. I didn't know what signals to look for. I didn't know the difference between infatuation, lust, and genuine caring that might someday evolve into love.

Once more, I had to lean on the old bromide: "Easy does it." I practiced patience. I learned to respect my date's needs. Dating a widow meant I had to appreciate that her grief and recovery were just as problematic for her as mine were for me.

There are no training programs for the newly widowed. We're on our own. The only available route to take is on-the-job training. Support groups do exist—peer-to-peer, professionally run, church-sponsored, and ad hoc. Funeral homes also sponsor support groups and grief assistance programs. While that may seem a bit macabre, it is not as weird as one might think. After all, who sees us when death hits us between the eyes? The folks who prepare our spouses for final disposition, as the euphemism goes.

When Annie's brother Jim passed away, I visited the website of the Costello-Runyon Funeral Home in Iselin, New Jersey, to post a condolence message.

When I clicked on a heading labeled "Grief Support," I found a treasure trove of help, available at no cost to anyone who chose to access the funeral parlor's home page. Bear in mind: This is one funeral home in one state.

Even so, the site listed grief support groups with contact information for a wide range of audiences: widows/widowers, young widows, recently bereaved, parents, Christian-based bereavement groups, single senior women, those suffering loss of a child/fetus, relatives of suicides. Other groups focused on those dealing with the death of a police officer, a victim of a drunk driver, and someone whose relative or friend was a victim of a homicide.

This list is not to be taken lightly. All these groups reach out to people who have undergone terrible, painful loss. Their pain may not resemble yours. For them, it is real, deadly serious, and life-changing in a major way.

Grief Word Library headed the second menu under "Grief Support." Most, if not all, selections in the area were written by Alan Wolfelt, Ph.D., an expert on grief and loss who serves as Director of the Center for Loss and Life Transition and is on the faculty at the University of Colorado Medical School's Department of Family Medicine.

The Costello-Runyon site featured two articles by Dr. Wolfelt: "The Journey Through Grief" and "The Mourner's Bill of Rights."

Besides these major articles, the web site listed 64 additional pieces by Dr. Wolfelt under such headings as: "Helping Yourself with Grief," "Helping Others with Grief," "For and About Grieving Children and Teenagers," and "Funerals, Memorials, Cremation, and Related Topics."

Brown Funeral Home in Martinsburg, West Virginia, would have been the service provider if Annie's death, bereavement arrangements, and burial had been more traditionally handled. Their website offers a slightly shorter list of similar articles about coping with grief and loss. It also provides a list of support resources and how to contact them.

Hastings Funeral Home in Morgantown, West Virginia, where Ann Gephart and I muddled through Annie's cremation and disposition arrangements, offers a somewhat smaller selection of articles by a still different author. The website has no list of groups that the surviving kin and friends can contact.

I wish I had known about these helpful sites when Annie died. I didn't. I went through on-the-job training. I suspect that most of us, even with the help of compassionate, experienced funeral directors, may be left with an inbox full of stuff and no clue about how to deal with it.

Chapter 27

My Foray into Domestic Arithmetic

I was clueless. If there's such a thing as mathematical dyslexia, I've got it. I hate math, can't do arithmetic, have eyes that glaze over at the mere mention of algebra or trigonometry. After Annie died, when I saw the checkbook, the bills that needed paying, and the retirement assets that needed oversight, I became almost catatonic.

My helplessness around family finances had become clear shortly after Annie and I got married and merged our bank accounts. I had originally managed the checkbook. After all, finances are a guy thing, right? One day the statement got so messed up that Anne dared to challenge my accounting skills.

"If you're so good, you do it."

"I will!"

She did—far better than I could.

In her OCD style, Annie balanced the checkbook to the last penny, checked every credit card statement, challenging me to account for why I might have spent $47.92 at a Mapco in Buchanan, Virginia. (I had gotten gas while driving to Auburn, Alabama, to visit my daughter.) Of course, I had forgotten all about that expense.

As the years passed, Annie continued to pay the bills, kept track of checking and savings accounts, and find ways to save money that was beyond my ken.

I would tease my wife, claiming she was a pharaoh in a prior life. She loved to build things: garages, dining rooms, porches, and decks. I didn't. Some of this was a reluctance to live up to my armpits in sawdust. Some was fear of financial insecurity.

Before undertaking a major project, our conversations would go something like this:

Annie, "We need a garage."

Me, "OK. Let's build a one-car garage." (We had only one car at the time.)

She, "No. We need a two-car garage."

Me, "How are you gonna pay for it?"

She, "I'll find the money."

End of conversation.

We compromised and built a two-car garage. Before much time had passed, we had a second car. Annie even had the contractor build a garage big enough to store rakes, shovels, my rarely used tool bench, and her gardening supplies. My conclusion: Never get into a debate with a wife who has more street smarts than you.

Annie's death left me numb. Her desk left me befuddled. The drawers contained our checkbook, about five years' worth of bank statements, a stack of credit card receipts, and some financial papers I couldn't even identify.

What's a poor widower to do?

Two people rescued me.

My long-time friend and neighbor, Maria, was a whiz at things like bookkeeping, balancing checkbooks, paying bills— things incomprehensible to me.

Annie's brother Chris is an MBA and a retired CFO. He understands things like investments, 401Ks, IRAs, and cash flow.

Propped up by these caring, competent people, as if they were a pair of crutches, I muddled through to a point where I can now deal with bills, autopay, and checkbook balances.

Another key person in my fiscal recovery was the guy who managed Annie's and my pension assets. Mid Tilghman gave me an infallible rule-of-thumb for knowing whether I was sailing smoothly on the asset ocean or about to wreck on the shoals of financial disaster. I share his priceless advice:

"Print out your monthly bank statement. Make sure the auto-pays and auto-deposits have been taken care of, and the checks have cleared. Look at your final balance. If it goes up or stays the same, things are fine. If it goes down a little, look to see why. If it goes down a lot, call me, and we'll move some money into your bank account." Easy. Foolproof. Able to be understood even by yours truly.

Annie had paid the bills for most of our married life. She had set up auto-pay for most of our regular expenses. She was no fool, knowing that if the day ever came, as it did, when I had to man up and assume control of the family finances, I'd most likely screw things up.

Annie would occasionally sit me down like an arithmetical illiterate, and explain, "I've just put the pet insurance on auto-pay. OK?" I'd mumble, "Yeah sure," or something like it, as if I actually cared. Then I'd go back to watching *Jeopardy* or the Sunday golf or some other mind-numbing TV show. Then Annie died. It dawned on me that these lessons in family economics had been real, and I had probably pulled a D. Quickly and through trial and error, I came to appreciate the efficiency and convenience of automatic transfers from the bank to the provider of goods and services.

With Annie no longer around to ignore, my challenge had become to understand which accounts had autopay and which didn't. I also had to take the steps necessary to smooth out a few more wrinkles in the financial security blanket my practical wife had created for me.

I found that bankers, the federal credit union staff, credit-card companies, and a bevy of other providers could not have been kinder or more helpful. I had heard the horror stories of incompetent and indifferent personnel who made this difficult adjustment positively painful. That was not my experience.

I learned to be assertive, to refuse to back down, and to inform the obstinate gatekeeper that I understood his or her difficulties but that I needed help. I was amazed at how responsive people became when I gently asked for help and acknowledged their importance instead of treating them like hired hands and demanding immediate complete service. Honey is a better lubricant than vitriol.

Chapter 28

Aftermath

We're taking longer to die. Extended-care facilities today number 22,200. There are 3,700 hospices in the U.S. That doesn't include hospice workers who make house calls. Before we took out long-term care insurance, Mid Tilghman told Annie and me, "You don't need to insure against dying. You need to insure against living."

Prolonged dying puts stress on families as well as the terminal individual. I have never experienced this. My wife died 10 days after a catastrophic accident. Surgeons kept her in a coma in an intensive-care trauma unit.

If not knowing you're dying or not being able to communicate with the dying person for a relatively short time eases their situation, that's a blessing, I suppose. I'd have foregone the blessing for 10 days to hold my wife's hand and comfort her.

Because Annie believed in the importance of good communication in a marriage and gently brought me around to her point of view during more than four decades of living together, we had no outstanding issues, no unresolved matters, no need for do-overs in our relationship. Not that we didn't need them during our married years. We simply managed—mostly at her insistence—to resolve situations soon after they had occurred.

When grief hit me right between the eyes, I went through all kinds of changes, almost none of which I expected. Some, I suppose, were beneficial. Others, I could well have done without.

I couldn't eat. I didn't sleep very well. My thoughts were more muddled than usual. My memory became even more intermittent.

Most of the time, I didn't realize that these symptoms had any significance either medically or as a response to Annie's death. I just felt like I was having a crummy day. These symptoms did not surprise or blindside me. They blindside many of us. We need to realize that they are caused by grief, not happenstance.

I didn't even know that my grief would include a lack of energy. I just figured I didn't want to get out of bed, didn't want to clean the house, didn't want to empty the kitty litter. Several years later, I still didn't. Grief? Sloth? Who knows? Who cares? The result, for me anyway, is the same. For me, the answer has been: "Get off your butt and live your life, pal!"

What I had to do initially was force myself to suit up and start my day. As my favorite philosopher, Woody Allen, put it, "Ninety percent of life is showing up." However, be advised, no one else had the right to tell me to get off my butt. My grief was mine alone. I had to own it. I had to live it. No one has the right to inject himself or herself into our painful journey. It is up to each of us to figure out how to build a life that is missing half a partnership.

Bereavement is unpredictable, unfamiliar. I learned the hard way that the mourning process is made up of ups and downs. I learned that the by-products of grief could scare the dickens out of me, but they couldn't kill me and that I could learn to ride that roller coaster. I was sad. I couldn't sleep through the night. Several years later, I'm not so sad. I do laugh and experience joy. I still can't sleep worth a damn, but as a friend of mine used to say, "Nobody ever died from lack of sleep!" Yeah, right!

I felt lonely, isolated, and sad. So, I moved to Alabama to be near my daughter's family. That was therapeutic. Once I was in Auburn, at my daughter's urging, I deliberately set out to make a network of new friends—even though I didn't want to. As much as I felt like isolating, John Donne's words kept ringing in my ears, "No man is an island." I guess that's the price one pays for being an English major!

Family nurtured me. Friends accepted me and introduced me to new friends. I had to realize these folks were a gift. But I was on my own. I was alone. I was now half a couple. More accurately, I was a functional bachelor even though I hadn't known what that felt like for more than 43 years. Alone? No kidding and unavoidable. Lonely? Totally optional.

In less than a year, I met a wonderful lady whose own grief journey was almost as long as mine. We have learned to communicate our stories, to share our pain, and—yes—our joys. And we have learned that love can be the balm that heals or at least mitigates grief.

Some people get angry—at the deceased, at themselves, at those who should have "fixed" their broken loved one. I never got angry about Annie's death. Did that make me uncaring? Maybe. Mostly, I'm uncaring about things that don't directly affect me. When I lost Annie, I knew what had happened. I knew, maybe better than the medical professionals, because I had let her die.

When I was told as a senior in college that my dad had died, I denied that it had happened, very briefly. Then, I accepted the inevitable, very unwillingly.

When I was told Annie had her accident, I accepted the news, but I was numb, dumbfounded, and utterly confused. Ten days later, I had no problem accepting her death. After all, I had precipitated it by instructing the doctor to discontinue life support. I felt absolutely no guilt making this decision. Annie and I both knew neither of us wanted to be left in a non-responsive state. Death was a gift I owed her, and I gave it willingly. She would have done the same for me. Some folks see or speak to their dead loved ones. Arthur Conan Doyle spent a fortune trying unsuccessfully to communicate with his dead wife.

I have never experienced Annie's presence or heard her voice. I wished many times in those first few months that I could see her, hear her, or sense her. Others I know have had that experience. Psychiatrists blithely label such experiences "hallucinations" cooked up to help the bereaved cope. My answer as a non-professional is: Who are you to judge? Don't label something until you have walked that walk. We don't have all the answers—or any—of what lies beyond the curtain. Maybe we never will. So, let's not act as if we do.

Grief makes us do or not do things, some of them pretty weird. I have already mentioned how losing Annie has affected my sleep. Different people experience sleep issues in different ways. I have no trouble falling asleep. But I wake up and can't get back to sleep. As an old guy with a dicey prostate, I get up to pee and can't get back to sleep. Most mornings, I wake up early and lie in bed, unsuccessfully trying to doze off.

Figuring if you can't beat 'em join 'em, I now set my alarm for 6:30 a.m. Sometimes, even when I think I haven't been asleep, I get that morning jolt that can only come from a detested alarm. Go figure. Is it shallow sleep? Is it mild insomnia? Is it sleep apnea? I have no idea. I just wish I could sleep until 9:00 some morning, pets be damned!

For me, eating has seldom been a problem. Even during my divorce. Even at other crisis points in my life. If you cook it, I will come. Initially, I didn't eat and lost weight. Many months later, I have had to join a gym as sweaty testimony that grief does ease even though it doesn't disappear. Neither does poundage!

For my fellow newly minted bachelors, I would also suggest that a gym is also a place to expand your network of friends, male and female.

As part of grieving, I discovered, we're likely to become forgetful. For me learning that information was a consolation. I was beginning to think my brain had started to turn into tapioca! I do forget stuff; I do walk into a room and forget why; I do lose a name in the middle of discussing a movie or TV show. But I guess I'm not ready for a locked ward. Yet!

When Annie died, I hid out. I didn't want to see anybody, talk to anybody, or socialize with anyone, close friends or not. My withdrawal from the social whirlwind probably cost me a few friendships because I was not returning phone calls or accepting invitations. That's too bad—for me, and maybe for them.

I regret my behavior—but only to some extent. I had to—we all have to—grieve in our own way at our own pace. If friends can't acknowledge and accept that need, then sadly, we must learn to let them go. Most of the long-standing, deep friendships have survived my thoughtless, self-centered behavior. Had I not been strong enough—selfish enough? stubborn enough? —to withdraw and nurse my wounded psyche, I don't know how I would have survived.

They say we experience unexpected, inexplicable crying jags. I did. Still do. I cry at Subaru commercials, Lifetime Channel chick-flicks, and certain songs that I sing or hymns that the choir sings in church. If I could stop the crying, I would, but it sneaks up on me. Sometimes, I'm mature enough to accept the grief leaching out of my soul, to acknowledge that it is good. The fact is, though, I don't like to be seen in public as a blubbering old fool.

That's my symptomology of grieving. It's no fun, but then I don't think nature and evolution intended that it should be fun for *homo sapiens* to lose a mate. If we weren't so tightly bonded, why would our predecessors ever have wanted to go out and knock a wooly mammoth on the noggin for wife and kiddies? This is how we have evolved, how we are programmed by our DNA. Live with it. Love, lose, and lament—the dismal triad destined for those of us who mourn our dear ones.

Fortunately, we also possess a built-in forgetter. Humans don't remember bad pain. At least most of us don't. If we did, women would never have more than one child. Men would never have more than one tooth pulled. A clergyman I know called forgetfulness a gift of God. I don't know about the giftedness of forgetting. I do know that remembering less and less as time passes has enabled me to heal and begin to move on.

Chapter 29

Final Thoughts

Dear Fellow Widowers,
  I know the journey you're taking. Maybe I'm a few paces—or many—further along. I can't fix you. I wouldn't try to talk you out of forging your own path. I wouldn't belittle—or exaggerate—what you're going through.
  Your loss is yours. Your grief is yours. Your mourning is unique to you. I acknowledge that. I respect it. I have been where you are, or someplace like it. I have slowly emerged from that dark place in which you feel trapped.
  I have no answer. You must find your own. I do have a few suggestions: Shut down if you must. But don't stay shut down. Withdraw to nurse your pain. But don't refuse to come back into the sunlight. Suit up and show up—when you feel ready. Know that the return trip is one of fits and starts—two steps forward, one step backward. That's OK. That's how I got where I am on my return journey. That's how all of us widowers get where we're going.
  Keep trudging at your own pace. At some point, healing will set in. You will come out on the other side of this dark cloud. When you do, I and others like me wait to welcome you.

Triptych II

Healing

I came to Alabama,
no expectations, no hope.
The shards of my life lay with Annie's urn
in a small plot in a small churchyard in West Virginia.

I suppose she wasn't really there,
just as I wasn't sure I was really here.
I was in Auburn because I really didn't know where else to be.

The Woods was my home so long as Annie made it habitable.
She died and my at-home-ness in West Virginia died with her.
The focal point of my life had disappeared. My nurturing
community, twenty-plus years of friendship in West Virginia,
had not deserted me.
I had abandoned the community, run away from home, gotten
outta Dodge.

I was looking for a new locus, a new home, a new place to
belong.
Why?
With Annie gone, I was left with half a life, partial belonging,
fragmented fellowship.
Lincoln, echoing Jesus, said, "A house divided against itself
cannot stand."
Obviously not Lincoln or Jesus, I was the house divided: One
foot in West Virginia, and one foot in Annie's grave.
This could not be.

I could not be the schizophrenic incarnation of my former life.
Hoping to heal my divided state,
I sought unity, repair, renewal in the only place where I had
any expectation of success—
in Alabama, with a family to nurture my brokenness.
Would it work?
Would my expectations be met?
I guessed I would find out sooner or later.
Sooner was my hope.

Rebuilding

How do you rebuild a life?
Does Lowes Home Improvement sell a handyman's manual:
"How to Rejoin the Pieces of a Broken Heart after Your Wife
Dies"?
For forty years I have clung to a copy of the *Reader's Digest
Complete Do-it-yourself Manual.*
This volume has helped me unclog toilets, hang
Venetian blinds, mount ceiling fans, build flower beds.
Reader's Digest had an answer for every problem, a solution to
any challenge that fell across my path.

Where were Lowes and *Reader's Digest* when I really needed
them?
No one could tell me how to mend my brokenness when Annie's
death shattered our marriage.
No publisher offered a method to piece together my splintered
life.
I had an option, one Annie had mentioned many times:
Move to Alabama.

Claire, my daughter, could fix me or so I thought, or so Annie
must have thought.
Then, when I thought a little harder,
I realized that only time and I could fix me.
Healing was an inside job.

Family and friends have lives to live, jobs to do, kids to nurture.
We widowed are the odd ones out,
the unwillingly born runts of the litter.
I heard myself tell kin and kind friends,
"I need to get back into my life."
How right I was.

Auburn gave me exactly what I needed
to reclaim what I thought death had stolen from me:
Some reason to get out of bed each morning.
Something to live for. Someone to care for.

But healing was—and is—a process, not an event.
I didn't wake up one morning and say,
"I think I'll be healed today.

"This is the day I stop being sad.
"This is the day I forget that Annie's death crushed my soul."

The grief journey goes on,
but the healing goes forward—
not sooner; not later; but every day.

New interests, burgeoning skills, human contact
are the warp and woof
with which I am weaving my new life.
The tapestry is not complete.
It probably will never be finished.
But the picture, the promise, is slowly emerging.

I like what I see.

Renewal

"God writes straight with crooked lines."
The old Spanish proverb incarnates the eternal cosmic joke:
Life evolves randomly.
Love is just as dicey, just as unpredictable.

That life and love surprise us should be no surprise.
I was resigned to my fate, my karma.
Then life and love snuck in the window of my awareness
as I was looking out the door of reduced expectations.

"You two need to talk," our instructor said,
at the end of the last class on Appalachian short stories.
The attractive lady of a certain age sitting next to me said
nothing.
"Why?"
"Because she lost her husband, a month after you lost your
wife."

Suddenly, I was alert.
Suddenly, I was interested.
Suddenly, I was engaged.

It seemed this woman had walked my walk.
She had carried, was carrying, a sorrow like mine.
Maybe I could hear her tale and learn from it.
Maybe she would listen to my painful journey
and soothe it with the balm of her sympathy.

We met. We shared. We found solace in each other's grief.
She couldn't remove my loss.
I couldn't remove hers.
But we learned over time that we could heal each other.
We learned that caring and gradual burgeoning love could salve
the breaks in our hearts, the pain of loss we carried.

There is a balm in Gilead to heal the wounded soul:
It is love.
We found it.
We gave it to each other.
It is often the only gift the bereaved can share.

Appendix 1

Complicated Grief

While I have no direct experience of complicated grief, M. Katherine Shear, M.D., has presented a good summary of this condition and its treatment methods in the journal of Bereaved Care, 2010, Jan. 1, pages 10-14. For your reference, the full title of her article is *Complicated grief treatment, the theory, practice and outcomes.*

Folks with complicated grief are stuck in a morass from which they can't free themselves. They need help, and specialize help is available. Dr. Shear highlights the difference between routine mourning and the painful box people find themselves in who experience the syndrome known as "Complicated Grief." She explains, "[M]ost people find a way to accept and integrate the unwanted reality of the death and restore their capacity for enthusiasm, joy, and satisfaction. Sometimes, . . . complicated grief develops. People suffering from complicated grief are caught in a seemingly endless cycle of acute grief and need help to find their way forward."

I'm just a sad guy who is probably no more neurotic than your next-door neighbor. While my knowledge of psychology is about as extensive as my grasp of astrophysics, I'm convinced that, if you are seriously in the dumpster because you can't figure out how to live your life following the death of someone close to you, if you are in a deep depression you can't seem to get out of, or if you want to harm yourself or others, seek professional help. Fast.

If your arm were broken, you'd see an orthopedist. If your heart and psyche are broken, you may need to see a mental health professional. If your soul is broken, see a member of the clergy, preferably someone with training as a pastoral counselor. There is no shame or guilt in seeking help for complicated grief.

You don't have to stay broken. With the proper help, it is possible to reach a point where you become stronger at the broken places. You can join the ranks of those who have not only survived but have gone on to rebuild their lives. Most of us do it, with or without outside assistance. Recovery is not easy, but it is possible.

Most of us learn to deal with grief—to accept what we can't change and to incorporate the pain of loss into who we are and what we will become. But we are never cured. We survive. Maybe we grow. But grief becomes part of us, a permanent part.

Me, I'm just a journeyman mourner. My wife died. It broke my heart. I tried, mostly through trial and error, to keep on keeping on. I am not depressive. I have never been suicidal. But I have been brokenhearted; I have been sad beyond anything I could have anticipated; I still have lousy days and parts of days when my loss comes back and hits me like a sledgehammer.

If your grief goes beyond this level of awfulness, please seek professional assistance.

Appendix 2

The Shape of a Broken Heart

People do die of a broken heart, according to WebMD. The Japanese call broken heart syndrome *Takotsubo syndrome*.

A *tako-tsubo* is a pot that's used in Japan for catching sea creatures. When Japanese researchers looked at images of people's hearts suffering from broken heart syndrome, they noted that the left ventricle had taken on an unusual shape resembling the fishing pot.

During an episode of the condition, the heart muscle can be so profoundly affected that it can't pump blood out to the body strongly enough. As a result, the patient may develop heart failure. This can be life-threatening, according to cardiologist Ilan Shor Wittstein, M.D., of Johns Hopkins Medical School.

The symptoms are so similar to those of a traditional heart attack—chest pain, shortness of breath, arm pain, and sweating—that paramedics and even many ER doctors can't tell the difference, he says. Because traditional heart attacks can be triggered by stress as well, he recommends that sufferers shouldn't take any chances when dealing with such cases:

"If you're at home having chest pain, you shouldn't question whether this could be stress cardiomyopathy just because you're going through a stressful period. The take-home message is to get to the hospital and let the doctors find out which one of these you're having."

Clues that may help lead your doctor to the right diagnosis are your age and gender. More than 90% of cases reported thus far have been in women. It's especially common after menopause. Some research suggests that about 2% of people who seem to be having a heart attack actually have broken heart syndrome. Among women, the number may be higher than 5%, Wittstein tells WebMD.

About the Author

Bill Wilson has been a professional communicator for more than fifty years. He has written or ghost-written six books, numerous magazine articles, columns, newsletters, speeches, radio public service announcements, and congressional testimony.

He holds a BA in Philosophy and an MA in English. As an accredited public relations professional (APR) and certified association executive (CAE), Bill has conducted strategic communications audits, media training, and press tours. He has also developed and taught numerous professional development programs for public relations and marketing staff. He was an adjunct instructor in the English Department of Northern Virginia Community College.

On August 14, 2015, Anne, Bill's wife of 41 years, was severely injured in an automobile accident. A week later, Anne was taken off life support. She expired on August 24 at Ruby Memorial Hospital in Morgantown, West Virginia.

In November 2016, Bill relocated to Auburn to be closer to family. Shortly thereafter, he joined OLLI (Osher Lifelong Learning Institute) at Auburn. He serves as chair of OLLI's Advisory Council and on OLLI's Promotion and Publicity Committee. He has lectured on widowhood at OLLI Wisdom Wednesdays and is a member of the Auburn Poetry Salon.

Endnotes

Poem for the Living. Theodora Kroebler. Personal words written for her obituary, March 24, 1979. No evidence of copyright. If one becomes available, copyright will be included in the next printing.

On Grief and Grieving, Finding the Meaning of Grief Through the Five Stages of Loss, Elizabeth Kubler-Ross and David Kessler, p. 230.

Complicated grief treatment, The theory, practice and outcomes. M. Katherine Shear, M.D., Professor of Psychiatry, Columbia University School of Social Work. The Journal of Bereavement Care, 2010, Jan. 1, pages 10-14.

The Shape of a Broken Heart. "Broken Heart Syndrome' Mimics Heart Attack." Ilan Wittstein, M.D., WebMD, Feb. 9, 2005.